PART OF THE Lizzy Albright COLLECTION

Granny's 1930 Sampler
Ricky Tims

The Pursuit of a Dream

Ricky Tims

Copyright © 2020 by Ricky Tims
Library of Congress Control Number: 2020912142

Publisher
Autumn Rock Publishing. All rights reserved under International and Pan-American Copyright Conventions. No part of this publication may be reproduced, distributed, or transmitted in any form or by any means, including photocopying, recording, or other electronic or mechanical methods, without the prior written permission of the publisher, except in the case of brief quotations embodied in critical reviews and certain other noncommercial uses permitted by copyright law. For permission requests, contact the publisher. Copying is only permitted for personal use by the owner of this book in order to make copies of necessary templates for making this quilt. At no time should multiple copies beyond what is required be distributed.

Editor Kathryn Patterson
Graphic Design Joyce Robinson
Photography Ricky Tims
Quiltmakers Cyndi McChesney (lead), Linda Kiniston, Sylvia McChesney, Martha Powers-Nosal, Winnie Soester, PJ Stephanson
Hand quilting Sarah Miller

www.lizzyalbright.com

ISBN 978-1-7352986-1-0
First edition printing, July 2020.
1-2020 ARP

Printed in the USA

CONNECTING GENERATIONS

In 2008, my good friend Kat Bowser presented me with the idea to create a children's book based on a little girl and her granny who was a quilt maker. As Granny taught her granddaughter (who we called Lizzy) the names of various quilt blocks, the little girl's imaginative mind raced with ideas and she made up stories. For example, a log cabin could become Sunbonnet Sue's house. Next door, an old maid might spend most of her time working on puzzles. A mariner's compass was needed to help the flying geese to avoid the impending storm at sea.

The crux of the concept was to follow up the story with a series of patterns that would be accessible for children. If we could connect the generations via a story, perhaps a new generation of quilters would be born—along with a series of companion products. It was a great idea, but due to...well... life, that idea was tabled.

In September 2017, Kat approached me about the possibility of reviving Lizzy. As things were shifting and changing in my own world, the idea of publishing a series of books seemed plausible—and fun! I asked Kat to write something—which she did. When I received the short story, it dawned on me that a picture book for kids was not going to be our first course of action. I told Kat, "We are not writing a children's book. We are going to write a full-scale fantasy novel!"

Over the next several months we met to work on the general synopsis. It wasn't too long before all of the main ideas were in place. It was a true labor of love for two novice novelists. When I was stumped trying to develop

a particular scenario, Kat and I would collaborate and come up with plausible solutions.

Lizzy Albright and the Attic Window is not a story about a quilt, but it is inspired by a quilt. Lizzy is ten years old in our story. She is celebrating her tenth birthday on Christmas Eve 1964. In the attic of the McHale family mansion, Lizzy discovers an heirloom sampler quilt which had been made by her Granny. She learns that Granny made it during the Great Depression.

I designed Granny's 1930 Sampler to be the inspiration for characters and other elements in the story. Not all of the blocks in this quilt are used in this story because we anticipate there will be sequels that can feature additional quilt blocks. If you haven't yet read *Lizzy Albright and the Attic Window*, please make it a point to do so—and do it with family. The story is appealing to all generations.

Back to the original goal…to create a story that has the potential to bring along a new generation of quilters. This had to be the first quilt. It's not your typical first quilt project for young sewers. But as you progress through making this quilt, you will find that I have simplified some things that will make the experience as easy as possible. There are plenty of kid-friendly blocks in this quilt. Going forward, we can now begin to create quilt patterns and quilting curriculum targeted to the young quilter. If you are an experienced quilter, they will appreciate your guidance.

Both Kat and I look forward to hearing your success stories.

—*Ricky Tims*

ABOUT THE AUTHOR

Ricky Tims has enjoyed a long and diverse career that coalesced from a variety of creative art forms. He is well-known in the international quilt industry as a TV host, best-selling author, teacher, award-winning quiltmaker, fabric designer, inspirational speaker, and live performance entertainer. He was selected as one of the Thirty Most Distinguished Quilters in the World. The readers of *Quilter's Newsletter Magazine* voted him (in a three-way tie with Alex Anderson and Karey Bresenhan) as the Most Influential Person in the Quilting Industry. The popular national television news show *CBS News Sunday Morning* featured him as one of their profiles.

Ricky, a gifted musician since early childhood, is a pianist, conductor, composer, arranger, music producer, and performing artist. With the publication of *Lizzy Albright and the Attic Window*, he adds novelist to his long list of creative endeavors. Ricky was born and raised in North Texas, but now resides on a remote mountain not far from the small town of La Veta in Southern Colorado.

DEDICATION

To my late Granny, Bertie Marie Newsom (1908-1993), for her unfailing faith and encouragement, and to all grandparents who selflessly guide and spoil their own grandkids.

Designed by Ricky Tims

Contents

The Pursuit of a Dream 2

Blocks Overview 5

Getting Started 6
- *Kits Ordering Information* 7
- *Books Ordering Information* 7

The Fabrics 8
- *Attic Window Collection* 8
- *Cedar Chest Collection* 9

Yardage 10
- *Quilt Size* 10
- *Supplies* 10
- *Important Cutting Notes* 10

Techniques 12
- *Traditional Piecing* 12
- *Oversized Piecing/Trimming Guides* 12
- *Foundation Paper Piecing (FPP)* 14
- *Appliqué* 16
- *English Paper Piecing (EPP)* 17

Quilt Assembly 118
- *Fabrics Needed* 118
- *Cutting* 118
- *Quilt Center* 120
- *Diamond Inner Border* 122
- *Flying Geese Outer Border* 124
- *Border Corner Units* 126

The Blocks

1. *Doves in the Window* 18
2. *Dresden Plate* 20
3. *Mariner's Compass* 22
4. *Jacob's Ladder* 24
5. *Old Maid's Puzzle* 26
6. *Churn Dash* 28
7. *Storm at Sea* 30
8. *Postage Stamp* 33
9. *Lemoyne Star* 34
10. *Snail's Trail* 36
11. *Double Pinwheel* 39
12. *Square in a Square* 40
13. *Robbing Peter to Pay Paul* 42
14. *Scottie Dog* 44
15. *Double Nine-Patch* 48
16. *Sawtooth Star* 51
17. *New York Beauty* 52
18. *Ohio Star* 56
19. *Rail Fence* 58
20. *Pickle Dish* 60
21. *Puss in the Corner* 63
22. *Sunbonnet Sue* 64
23. *Friendship Star* 66
24. *Kaleidoscope* 68
25. *Hunter's Star* 70
26. *Bear Paw* 72
27. *Spools* 74
28. *Pineapple* 76
29. *Fifty-Four Forty or Fight* 78
30. *Honey Bee* 80
31. *Moon Over the Mountain* 82
32. *Tumbling Blocks* 86
33. *Grandmother's Flower Garden* 88
34. *Grandmother's Fan* 90
35. *Delectable Mountains* 94
36. *Courthouse Steps* 98
37. *Dutchman's Puzzle* 100
38. *Birds in the Air* 102
39. *Double Wedding Ring* 106
40. *Log Cabin* 110
41. *Broken Dishes* 112
42. *Kansas Dugout* 114

  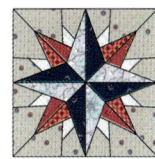  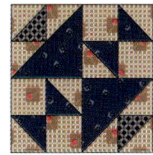 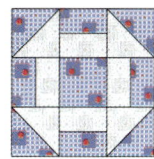

1 Doves in the Window **2** Dresden Plate **3** Mariner's Compass **4** Jacob's Ladder **5** Old Maid's Puzzle **6** Churn Dash

   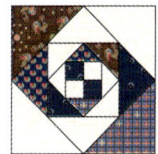  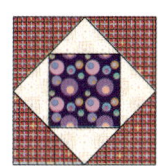

7 Storm at Sea **8** Postage Stamp **9** LeMoyne Star **10** Snail's Trail **11** Double Pinwheel **12** Square in a Square

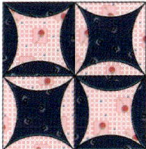 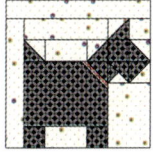 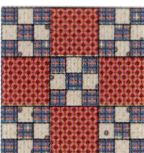   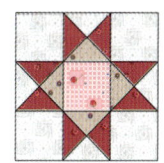

13 Robbing Peter to Pay Paul **14** Scottie Dog **15** Double Nine-Patch **16** Sawtooth Star **17** New York Beauty **18** Ohio Star

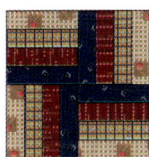     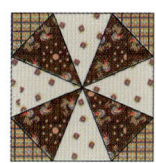

19 Rail Fence **20** Pickle Dish **21** Puss in the Corner **22** Sunbonnet Sue **23** Friendship Star **24** Kaleidoscope

  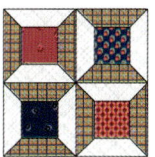  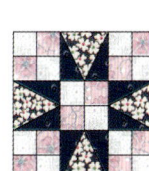 

25 Hunter's Star **26** Bear Paw **27** Spools **28** Pineapple **29** Fifty-Four Forty or Fight **30** Honey Bee

  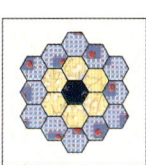   

31 Moon Over the Mountain **32** Tumbling Blocks **33** Grandmother's Flower Garden **34** Grandmother's Fan **35** Delectable Mountains **36** Courthouse Steps

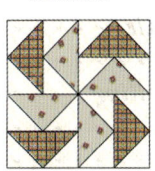 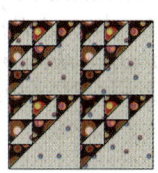    

37 Dutchman's Puzzle **38** Birds in the Air **39** Double Wedding Ring **40** Log Cabin **41** Broken Dishes **42** Kansas Dugout

Designed by Ricky Tims

Getting Started

Kit 1, Red and Tan

Kit 2, Navy and Yellow

Scottie dogs frolicking on boxes? Playful cherries on a grid? Discover how fancy singing roosters, traditional plaids, and fun flowers with fluffy marshmallows coordinate perfectly with bubbling orbs and floating squares. I created these two eclectic collections of vintage-style fabric designs specifically for this quilt. The prints are easy to mix-and-match, and will easily blend with other basics you may have on hand. The Lizzy Albright novel, the Lizzy Albright fabrics, and this quilt pattern book are only the start of part of a master plan for quilters and to bring youngsters to quilting. There are two kits available. The difference is only in the border and bottom attic window sashing. Watch the Lizzy Albright adventure grow and blossom.

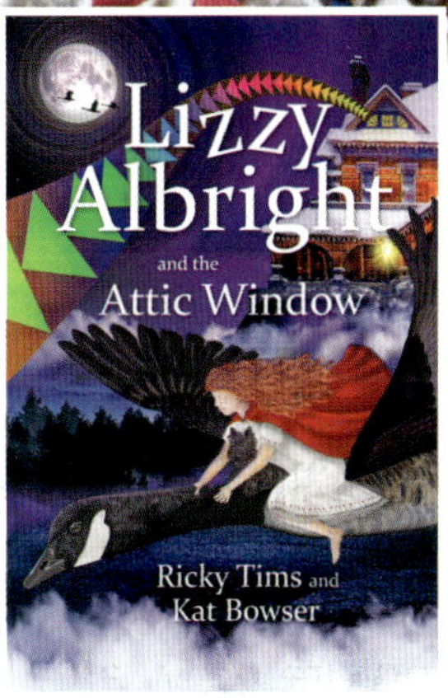

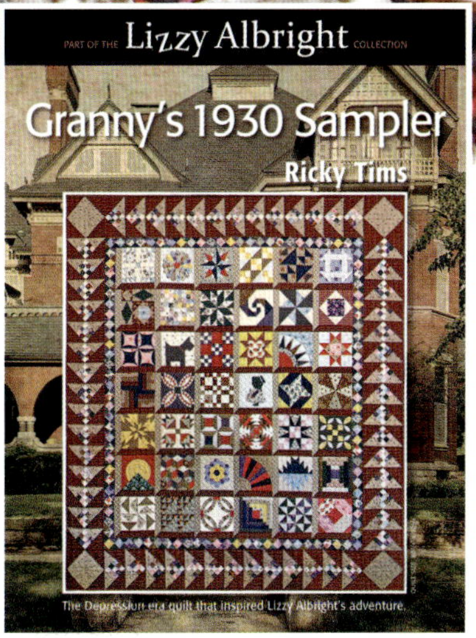

KITS, BOOKS, VIDEO TUTORIALS, AND OTHER LIZZY ALBRIGHT ITEMS

www.lizzyalbright.com
or
www.rickytims.com

Designed by Ricky Tims

The Fabrics

TWO COLLECTIONS COME TO LIFE

Because Lizzy's granny made this quilt in 1930, it was imperative that the fabrics in the quilt had a vintage appearance. I designed each fabric in the Attic Window and Cedar Chest collections based on motifs and patterns on fabrics in my antique collection. None of them are reproductions, but they do represent the typical designs and colors of that time period. The collection has been printed and produced by Benartex. Kits are available. For details, visit www.rickytims.com or www.lizzyalbright.com

Note: Fabrics are shown at 25% scale.

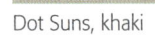

Attic Window

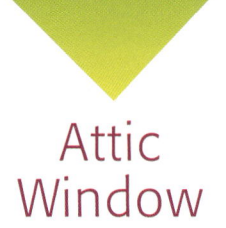
Scottie Dog on Boxes, red

Scottie Dog on Boxes, teal

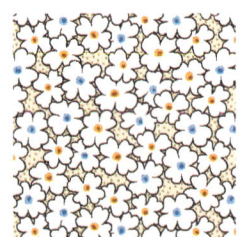
Posies, cream

Posies, navy

Dot Suns, cream

Dot Suns, khaki

Dot Suns, toast

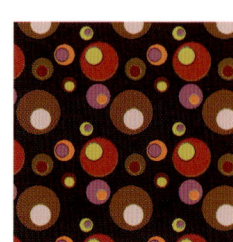
Bubbles, brown

Bubbles, green

Bubbles, purple

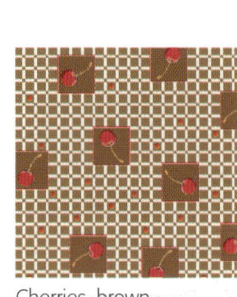
Diamond Lattice, black

Diamond Lattice, red

Cherries, brown

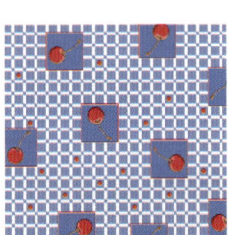
Cherries, blue

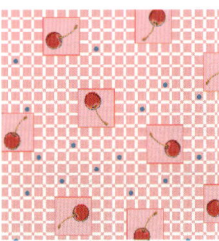
Cherries, pink

Pajama Squares, khaki

Pajama Squares, navy

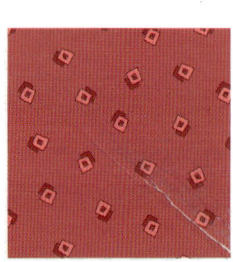
Pajama Squares, red

Cedar Chest

- Singing Rooster, brown
- Singing Rooster, cream
- Plaid, khaki
- Plaid, rose
- Circle Swirls, ecru
- Circle Swirls, gray
- Fun Flowers, pink
- Fun Flowers, yellow
- Fun Flowers, aqua
- Double Grid, blue
- Double Grid, brown
- Double Grid, red
- Rosebuds, burgundy
- Rosebuds, navy
- Lozenge, cream
- Lozenge, gray
- Line Dots, green
- Line Dots, red

Designed by Ricky Tims

Yardage

QUILT SIZE
81¼" x 90¾" (includes binding)

BLOCK SIZE
8" x 8" finished (8½" x 8½" raw edge to raw edge)

QUILT CENTER
57" x 66½" (57½" x 67" raw edge to raw edge)

YARDAGE

This project is meant to be approached as a scrap quilt, therefore yardage requirements are not given for each specific fabric used in the quilt. Instead, the piece size needed for each fabric used in a block is given at the beginning of that block pattern. However, several fabrics (those used for sashing strips, the 2 prominent prints in the outer border, binding fabric, and backing) are used in larger quantities:

Assorted prints (blocks, inner border, outer border nine-patch units)	20–22 yards total
Fabric for vertical (upright) sashing strips	1 yard
Fabric for horizontal sashing strips, outer border background, and binding	4 yards
Fabric for outer border light triangles and corner diamonds	1¼ yards
Backing fabric	7½ yards
Batting	90" x 99"

SUPPLIES

In addition to fabric, here are some recommended supplies for this project:

- - - Heat resistant template plastic
- - - Foundation paper
- - - Glue stick or fabric basting glue
- - - Light cardstock
    (for English paper piecing)
- - - Freezer paper

PREWASHING

It is your choice whether to prewash your fabrics or not. Please keep in mind that *if you do not prewash*, colors in the quilt may bleed upon first washing and you will also be in close contact throughout your project with whatever chemicals were used in the manufacture of the fabrics. *If you do prewash*, it will be necessary to iron all your fabric afterwards before cutting. I recommend the use of a good sizing or starch during the pressing to stabilize the fabric for cutting and sewing.

IMPORTANT CUTTING NOTES

Cut patches for vertical and horizontal sashing, the outer border, and binding first. Cutting instructions are on page 118. You will be able to use any leftover pieces of these fabrics in your scrap fabric selections for the blocks.

FABRIC SELECTION AND PLACEMENT

- - - To make the most authentic Granny's 1930s Sampler quilt, use the Lizzy Albright fabric collections, the colorway shown on the cover, and the block highlighted at the beginning of each block pattern.

- - - Or, choose from one of the three Color Options provided that also feature fabrics from the Lizzy Albright fabric collections.

- - - You could also use the Lizzy Albright fabrics and create your own variation.

- - - Choose your own fabrics and color placement.

Designed by Ricky Tims

Techniques

There are 5 main techniques used in making this quilt. *Traditional piecing* is done with either rotary-cut patches or patches cut using templates provided with the block pattern. *Oversized traditional piecing* involves making units from slightly oversized rotary-cut patches, and then trimming them to size using the provided Trimming Guides. In *foundation paper piecing*, patches are sewn to a paper foundation as they are added to each other for creating unusually-shaped units. *Appliqué* is used sparingly in this quilt, most notably in the Sunbonnet Sue block, but it is also suggested in some cases (for example, the New York Beauty block) for sewing curved units together. *English paper piecing* appears in only 2 cases, Tumbling Blocks and Grandmother's Flower Garden.

TRADITIONAL PIECING

Most patches used in traditional piecing are cut to size with rotary-cutting tools (rotary cutter, acrylic ruler, and self-healing cutting mat). In some cases, square patches are subcut either once or twice on the diagonal to make triangles. This symbol ◺ means cut a square patch diagonally once to make 2 half-square triangles (HSTs). This symbol ⊠ means cut a square patch diagonally twice to make 4 quarter-square triangles (QSTs).

Some patches of unusual size or shape are cut using templates, for example the A, C, and D patches in the Doves in the Window block (page 18). In these cases, template shapes are given with the block pattern. Trace these shapes onto template plastic and cut them out directly on the traced lines. Transfer any markings (match points, grain lines, etc.) to the plastic template. Now trace the template shape onto the right side of your fabric, transfer any match points, etc., and then cut out the fabric patch on the traced lines.

Once your fabric patches are cut as directed, sew them right sides together in the order given in the block pattern, using an accurate ¼" seam allowance.

OVERSIZED PIECING/ TRIMMING GUIDES

Because all the blocks in this sampler finish at 8" square, any block design based on a 3 x 3 grid (for example, Double Nine-Patch on page 48) requires

patches to be cut with templates, or patches or sewn units to be cut or made oversized and then trimmed. Trimming Guides are given in each block pattern where they are required, for example in the Jacob's Ladder block on page 24. Some of the Trimming Guides include light gray lines to indicate where to align the guide with the seams of a sewn oversized unit.

To use a Trimming Guide, make an accurate copy on plain paper. Cut the guide out on the outer lines, and then tape it to the wrong side of a clear acrylic ruler, aligning the corners. Center the guide on the patch or sewn unit, aligning any gray lines with seams. Use a rotary cutter to trim two adjacent sides, rotate the patch or unit, realign with the guide, and trim the remaining two sides.

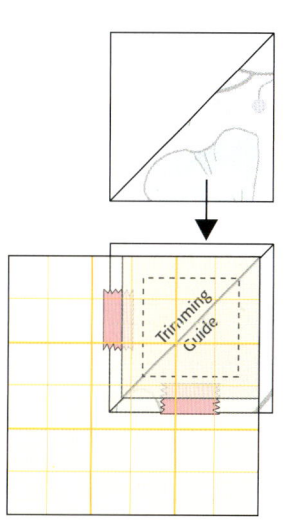
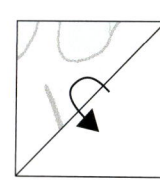
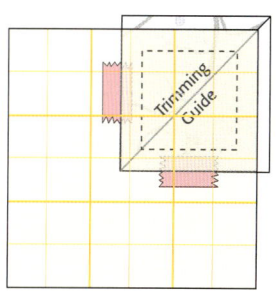
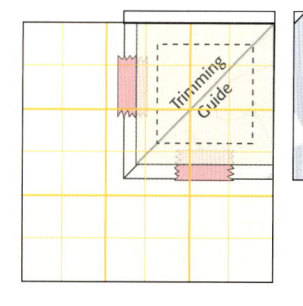
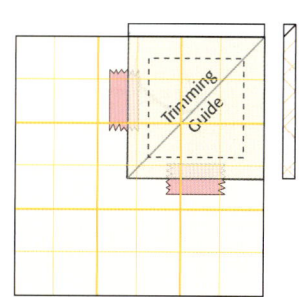
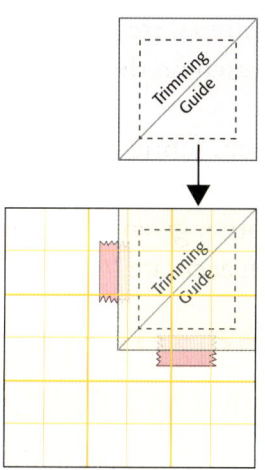
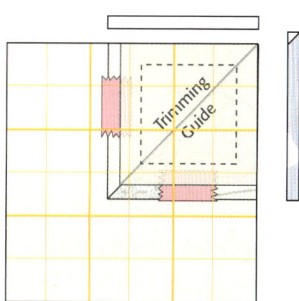
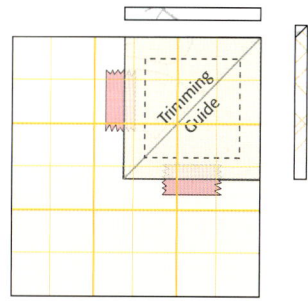

Align trimming template with ruler corner and tape to back of ruler.

Center and align grey lines on template with seams; trim.

Rotate patchwork, align template corner with corner; trim.

Designed by Ricky Tims

Techniques

FOUNDATION PAPER PIECING (FPP)

This technique allows for piecing unusually-shaped units, and also creates extremely accurate units and blocks. See the Mariner's Compass block on page 22 as an example. FPP is definitely worth adding to your quilting bag of tricks! Patches are sewn to a paper foundation, working on the unprinted side of the pattern. Directions for cutting fabric patches to use with this technique are included in each block where it is required. Generally, these patches are cut as squares or rectangles, but in some cases, patches are cut as oversized triangles to avoid fabric waste.

Begin by printing or tracing accurate copies of the foundation(s) as directed in the block pattern. You can use regular printer paper for this, but paper specifically designed for FPP is definitely a worthwhile investment and is easily available at your local quilt shop or online.

Once your foundations are ready, prepare your sewing machine. Set your stitch length slightly shorter than usual (generally 1.5-1.8mm); this helps perforate the paper as you sew to make removal of the paper easy later in the process. It also strengthens the seams.

The foundations include numbers to indicate the piecing order. Always begin by placing the fabric patch for area 1 on the unprinted side of the foundation, wrong side of fabric against the paper, completely covering area 1 and extending beyond each of the surrounding seam lines by at least 1/4". You may have to hold the paper and fabric up to a light source to be sure of placement, especially for darker fabrics. Once you are sure of placement, use a dab of glue stick to temporarily adhere the fabric patch to the unprinted side of the foundation.

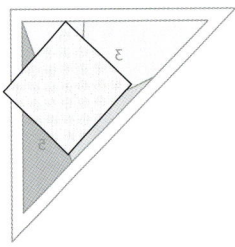
Glue backside of fabric 1 to unprinted side of foundation, generously covering area 1.

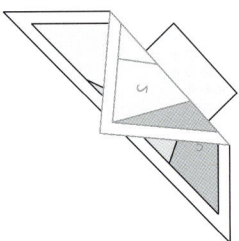
Turn over, and fold back foundation along seam line.

Turn the foundation printed side up and fold it back on the seam line between areas 1 and 2. Trim the seam allowance of the area 1 patch to 1/4" or slightly less (3/16"). Unfold the foundation.

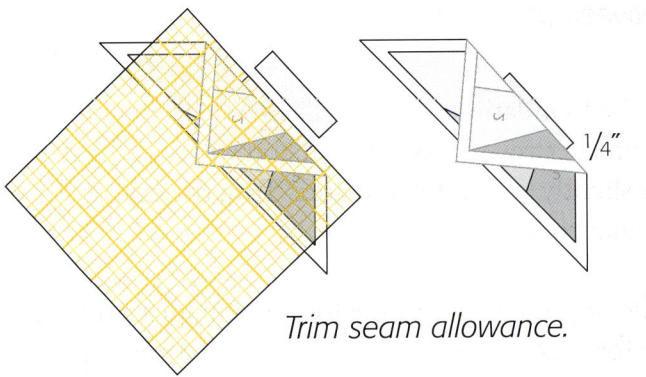
Trim seam allowance.

On the unprinted side of the foundation, place the fabric patch for area 2 right sides together on the area 1 fabric patch, aligning it with the trimmed edge of the area 1 patch.

Granny's 1930 Sampler: From the Lizzy Albright Collection

Pin in place, and then temporarily open the area 2 patch to make sure it completely covers area 2 and extends past it in every direction by at least ¼". Smooth the area 2 patch back in place.

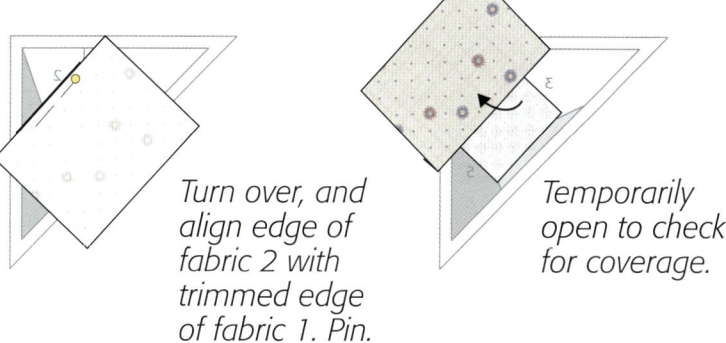

Turn over, and align edge of fabric 2 with trimmed edge of fabric 1. Pin.

Temporarily open to check for coverage.

Flip the foundation over, and sew directly on the seam line between areas 1 and 2. Start slightly before the line and finish slightly after the line as shown. Press the added patch open to cover area 2.

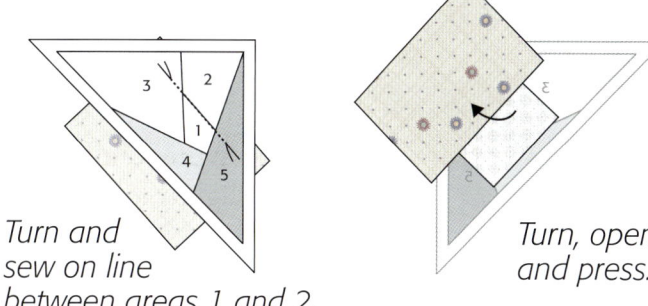

Turn and sew on line between areas 1 and 2.

Turn, open and press.

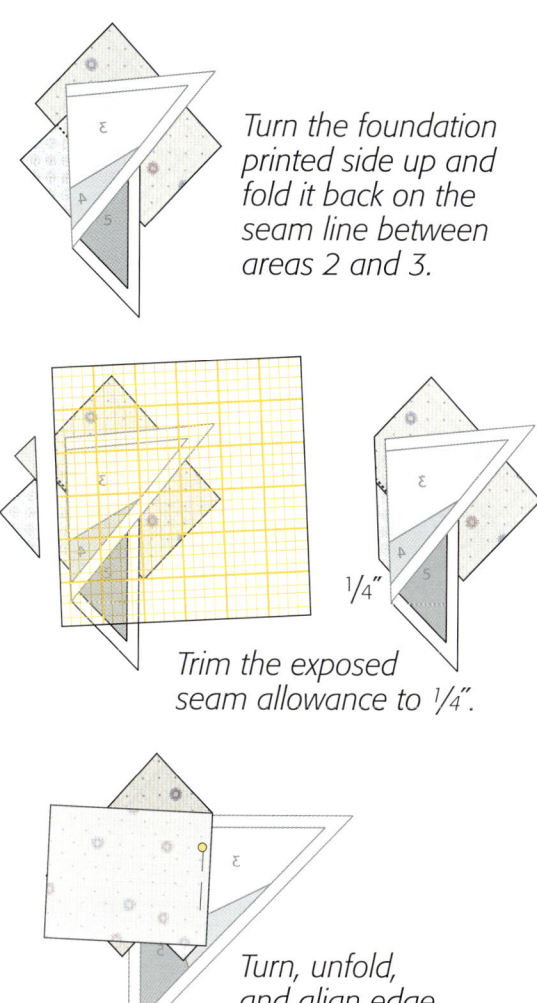

Turn the foundation printed side up and fold it back on the seam line between areas 2 and 3.

Trim the exposed seam allowance to ¼".

Turn, unfold, and align edge of fabric 3 with trimmed edge. Pin.

Turn the foundation printed side up and fold it back on the seam line between areas 2 and 3. You will need to tear the paper slightly at the stitched area. Trim the exposed seam allowance to ¼".

On the unprinted side of the foundation, place the fabric patch for area 3 right sides together on the area 2 patch, aligning it with the trimmed seam allowance. Pin in place, and then temporarily open the area 3 patch to make sure it completely covers area 3 and extends past it in every direction by at least ¼". Smooth the area 3 patch back in place.

Flip the foundation over, and sew directly on the seam line between areas 2 and 3. Press the added patch open to cover area 3. Repeat this process to add all the patches needed to cover the foundation.

Once the foundation is complete, trim the paper and fabric even with the outer lines. The individual block patterns provide direction for when to remove the paper from the backs of the units.

Designed by Ricky Tims

Techniques

APPLIQUÉ

There are many ways to add appliqué shapes to blocks – your quilt, your choice! However, my favorite technique by far, especially for a quilt with a vintage vibe, is an invisible blind stitch done by hand. This is also a great way to join curved units to each other, avoiding the sometimes-tricky process of machine-piecing curves.

To prepare shapes for hand appliqué, trace the pattern(s) onto heat-proof template plastic or a double-thick sheet of freezer paper (two sheets ironed together) and cut them out. Place the template(s) right side down on the wrong side of the selected fabric(s), trace, and then cut them out, adding approximately a 3/16″ turn-under allowance. This does not have to be exact; you can eyeball it.

Position the plastic or freezer paper template on the wrong side of the shape and apply starch or sizing to the turn-under allowance. Press it to the wrong side of the shape. Remove the template and press again.

Once all your shapes are prepared, arrange them on the block background as shown in the photos and diagrams. When you are pleased with the arrangement, apply small dots of fabric glue to the wrong sides of the shapes and firmly finger-press them to the background. Now your block is glue basted and ready to stitch.

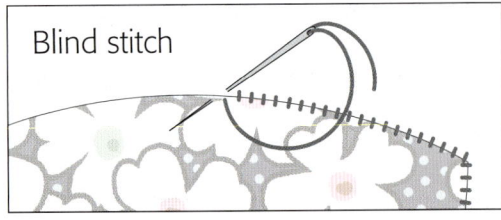
Blind stitch

Knot your thread and bring the needle up from the back of the block through the folded edge of a basted shape, catching just one or two threads. Push the needle down through the background next to where it came up through the shape. Take your next stitch in the same way, keeping stitches close together, approximately 10-12 stitches per inch. Continue all around any exposed edges of the shape; do not stitch any edges covered by another overlapping shape.

To finish stitching a shape, bring the needle to the back of the block, take a tiny stitch in the background fabric beneath the shape, leaving a small thread loop, bring the needle through the loop, and pull snug, creating a knot.

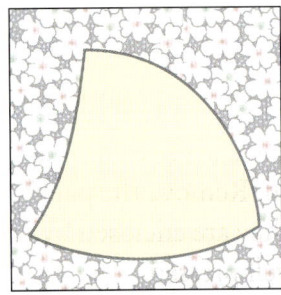 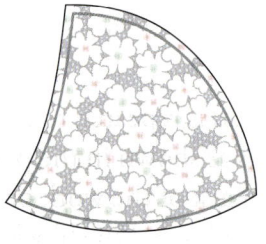 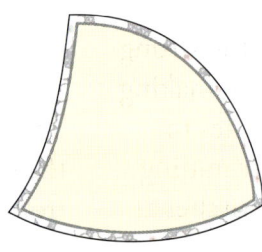 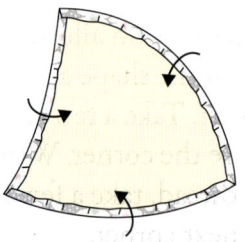

Granny's 1930 Sampler: From the Lizzy Albright Collection

ENGLISH PAPER PIECING (EPP)

This is a great technique for creating and joining complex-shaped patches such as diamonds (see Tumbling Blocks, page 86) and hexagons (as in Grandmother's Flower Garden, page 88). The stitching is done by hand, so it's relaxing and portable, great for passing time in waiting rooms and at kids' sporting events.

Start by printing or tracing template shapes onto light card stock or heavy paper. Cut the shapes out. Each can be used several times, so you don't need a separate paper template for every patch in the block or quilt.

Pin the template to the wrong side of the fabric patch. Trim around the template, leaving approximately 3/16″ turn under allowance on all sides.

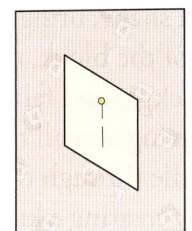
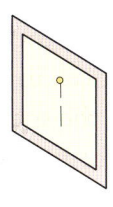

Fold the seam allowances to the wrong side of the shape at one corner, making a miter. Take a few small stitches to secure the corner. Without trimming the thread, take a few small stitches at the next corner.

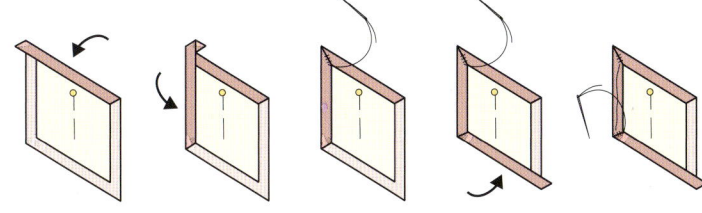

Some people stitch through the template as well as the fabric, but if you stitch only through the fabric, it's much easier to remove the paper template later.

Continue around the shape until all corners are securely basted. Trim the thread and remove the pins. Press the shape well.

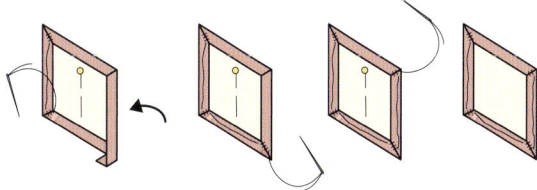

To join prepared shapes, place them right sides together, aligning edges to be joined. Using a knotted thread, take a stitch right at the corner, catching only a few threads of each shape. Take the next stitch about 1/8″ from the first, again catching just a few threads of each shape. Continue in this way until the end of the seam, take a few tiny stitches to secure, and trim the thread.

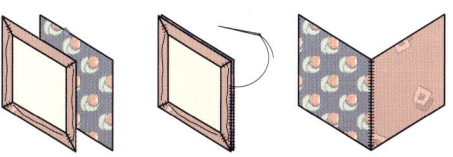

This process is repeated to create all the seams needed to join the shapes as shown in the pattern. Remove the paper shapes from the back of the work once they are enclosed by stitching on all sides and the block is well pressed.

Designed by Ricky Tims

1 Doves in the Window

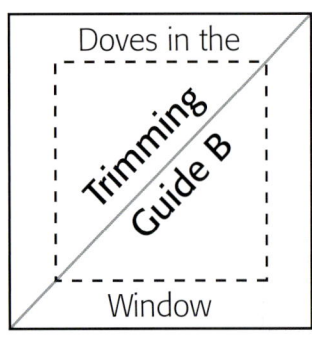

There are at least a dozen different quilt blocks commonly referred to by this name, which is a reference to the dove that returned to the window of Noah's ark, bearing an olive leaf as proof of life returning after the Great Flood. The *Ladies Art Company* featured this particular version of the block as early as 1895. Laura Ingalls Wilder, of *Little House on the Prairie* fame, wrote about a Doves in the Window quilt that she made. Doves are often the symbols for love, peace, and gentleness.

FABRICS NEEDED

Fabric 1 (small squares and triangle points): 8" x 12"
Fabric 2 (background): 9" x 13"
Fabric 3 (large squares): 7" x 7"

CUT

Fabric 1
    5 Template A
    8 squares 2¼" x 2¼" (B)
Fabric 2
    8 squares 2¼" x 2¼" (B)
    4 Template D
Fabric 3
    4 Template C

Instructions for using Trimming Guides are on page 12.

SEW

Draw a diagonal line on the wrong side of each fabric 1 or fabric 2 B square (whichever fabric is lighter). Place a fabric 1 and a fabric 2 B square right sides together with marked

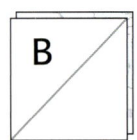 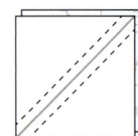 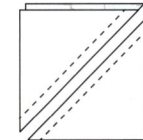  

∗ = B trimmed

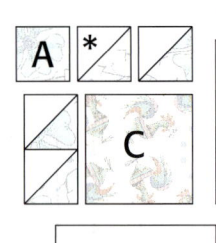 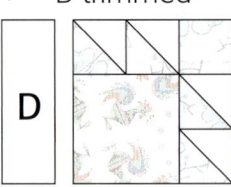

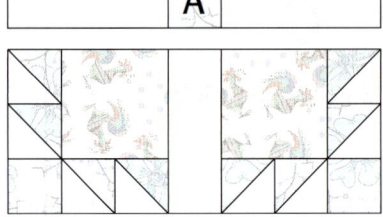

Doves in the Window Assembly

fabric on top. Sew ¼" from each side of the marked line. Cut apart on the marked line to make 2 pieced squares. Repeat to make 16. Press seams towards the darker fabric. Trim all the pieced squares to size using the Trimming Guide.

Referring to the Assembly diagram, sew together 4 pieced squares and 1 each A and C squares to make a quarter-block. Make 4.

Sew 3 rows using the 4 quarter-blocks, 4 D strips, and the remaining A square. Sew the rows together to complete the Doves in the Window block.

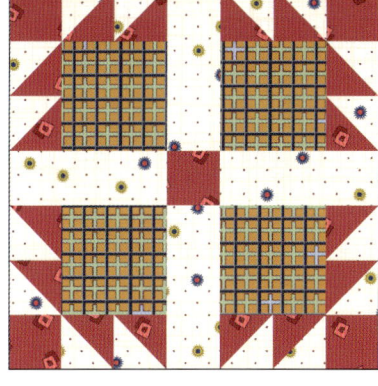

Doves in the Window Color Options

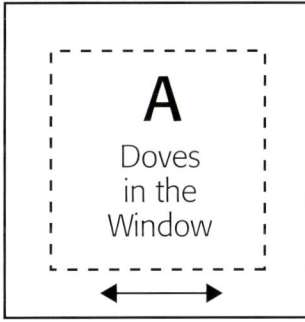

A
Doves in the Window

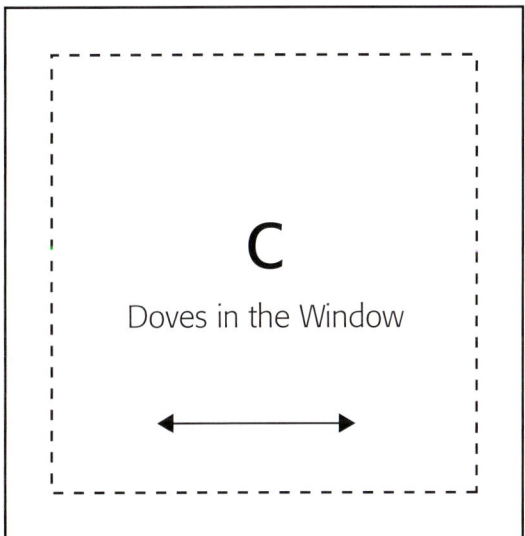

C
Doves in the Window

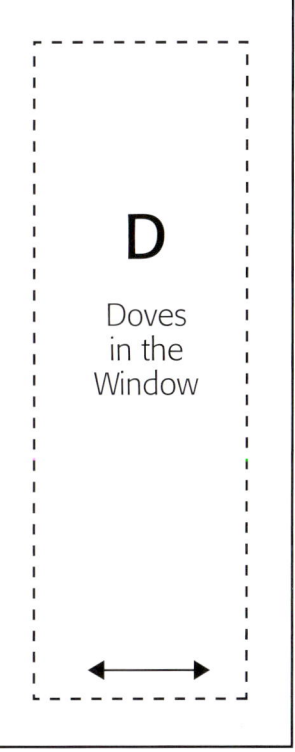

D
Doves in the Window

Designed by Ricky Tims   19

2 Dresden Plate

This pattern was extremely popular in the 1920s and 1930s. Earlier variations of the block were created by combining four Grandmother's Fan blocks. Other common names for the Dresden Plate block include Friendship Ring, Aster, Grandmother's Sunburst (the name it was published under in *Wallaces' Farmer* newspaper in 1928), and Dessert Plate.

FABRICS NEEDED

Fabric 1 (background): 9″ x 9″ (A)
Fabric Group 2 (plate): assorted prints totaling 8″ x 16″
Fabric 3 (plate center): 2″ x 2″

CUT

Fabric Group 2 – *cut a total of:*
  16 Template B
Fabric 3
  1 Template C

SEW

In this block, the "plate" is first pieced and then appliquéd to a slightly over-size background square. Once the appliqué is finished, the block is trimmed to size—perfect every time!

Mark dots on wrong side of each B shape as shown on template. Arrange 16 Bs in a pleasing manner. Sew together in pairs, starting each seam at the narrow end and stopping and backstitching a few stitches at dots. In the same way, sew pairs together and then sew units together to complete the plate.

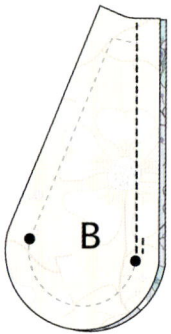
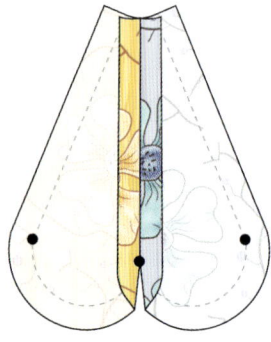

To make pressing guides, trace B shapes *without seam allowances* onto heat-resistant template plastic, light card stock, or a stack of 3 sheets of freezer paper pressed together. Cut out the B guides on the traced lines. Press the seams of the plate open. Place the pressing guides on the wrong side of the B patches and use spray starch and an iron to press under the curved edge of the plate ¼″. You can trim the curved edge of the fabric slightly to reduce bulk during pressing if needed. Pin or glue-baste the plate to the fabric 1 square, centering. Appliqué curved edge of plate to background square. Appliqué C circle to center of plate.

Dresden Plate Color Options

Add 3/16" turn-under allowance to C.

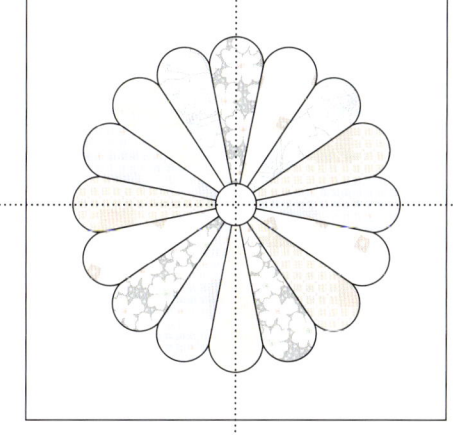
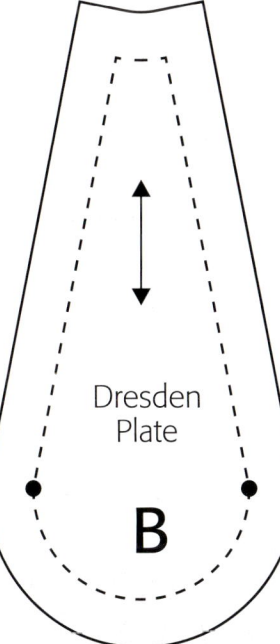
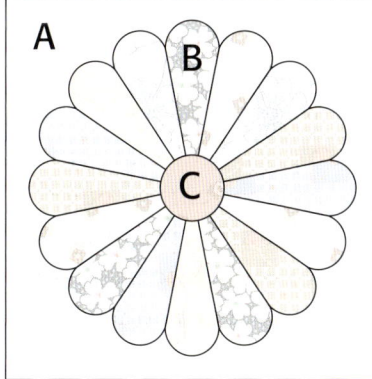

Dresden Plate Assembly

Trim block to 8½" square, centering the plate, to complete the Dresden Plate block.

FROM THE PAGES OF
Lizzy Albright and the Attic Window, Chapter 6

"This one is a Dresden Plate. Back in those days, a set of Dresden china was the envy of every bride. But when times got bad, it was much harder to afford a set of china…let alone, expensive Dresden china…so it became popular to make quilts with this design. Look at the wedges coming out from the center, can you see how the block resembles a fancy dinner plate?"

Lizzy nodded when she saw the similarities.

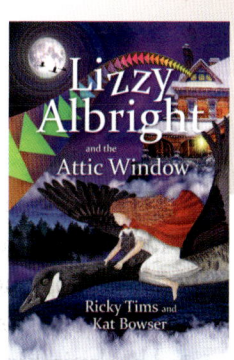

Designed by Ricky Tims

3 Mariner's Compass

There may be as many variations of the Mariner's Compass quilt block as there are stars in the sky! Patterns for blocks similar to this one were published as early as 1909, and home-drafted versions were popular even earlier. Find your own way to a beautiful quilt block with this simple foundation-pieced design, easy enough for beginners.

FABRICS NEEDED

Fabric 1 (small points): 6" x 6"
Fabric 2 (background): 7" x 20" or fat eighth (9" x 20-22" cut of fabric)
Fabrics 3 and 4 (medium points): 4" x 8" *each*
Fabrics 5 and 6 (large points): 6" x 12" *each*

SEW

Make 4 accurate paper copies each of foundations 1 and 2. Foundation piece 4 each of units 1 and 2, paying close attention to placement of fabrics in areas 4 and 5. Trim edges even with outer lines on foundation papers.

CUT

Fabric 1
    8 rectangles 1½" x 2" (area 1)
Fabric 2
    8 rectangles 2¾" x 3½" (area 3)
    8 squares 2½" x 2½" (area 2)
Fabrics 3 and 4 – *cut from each*:
    4 rectangles 1¾" x 3½" (area 4)
Fabrics 5 and 6 – *cut from each*:
    4 strips 2" x 5" (area 5)

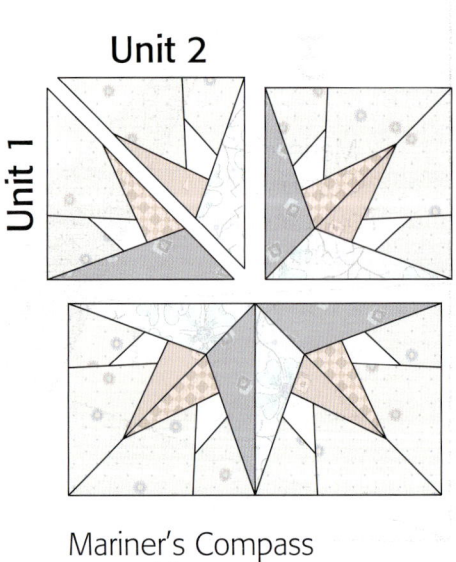

Mariner's Compass Assembly

Sew unit 1 and unit 2 together, matching lines on foundation papers, to make a pieced square. Press seam open. Make 4. Sew pieced squares together, pressing seams open, to complete the Mariner's Compass block.

Sew a line of stay stitching inside the outer seam allowance of the block (about 1/8″ from the raw edges). Carefully remove all foundation paper from the back of the block.

Mariner's Compass Color Options

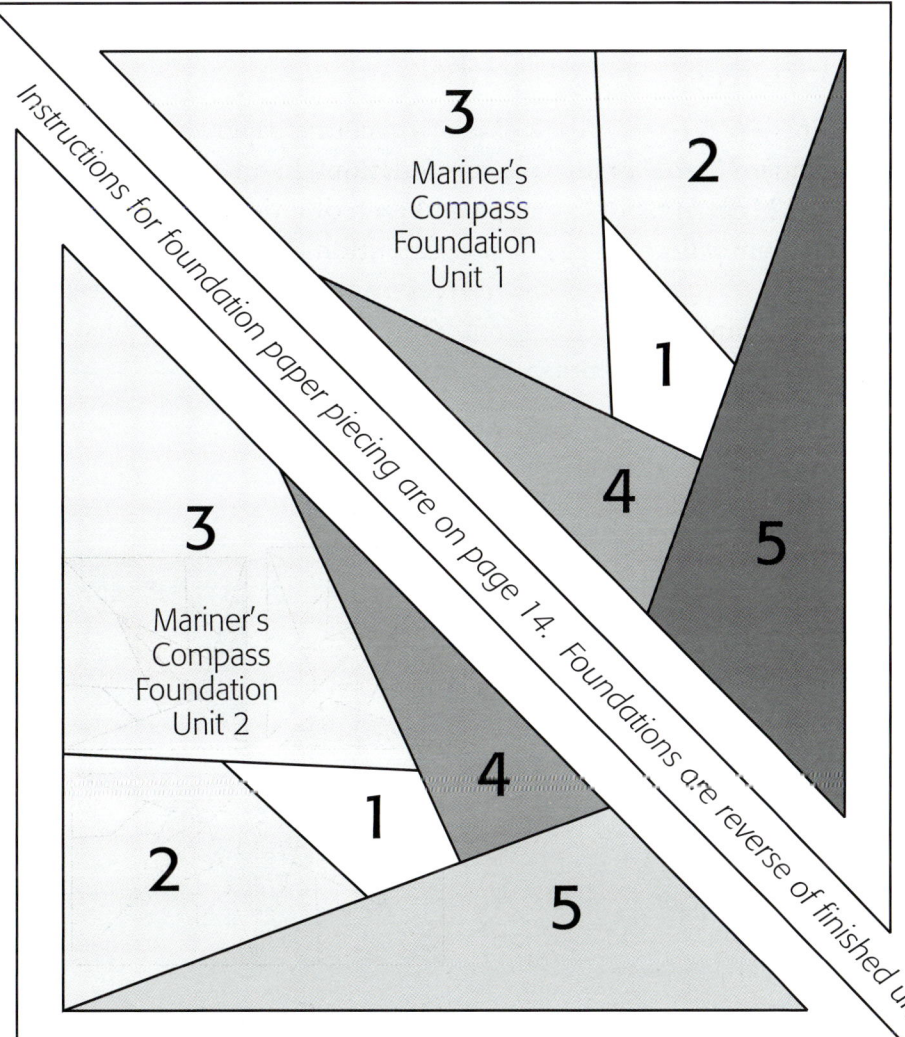

Designed by Ricky Tims

4 Jacob's Ladder

The name Jacob's Ladder, along with strong diagonal lines in this much-loved block, is a reflection of the biblical story in which Jacob dreams of a ladder used by the angels of God to ascend and descend between heaven and earth. Alternate names for this design include Railroad, Golden Stairs, Road to California, and Susie's Fancy, and published patterns date back at least as far as the late 1800s.

FABRICS NEEDED

Fabrics 1 and 2 (four-patches):
    5" x 11" *each*
Fabric 3 and 4 (triangles): 4" x 8" *each*

CUT

Fabrics 1 and 2 – *cut from each:*
    10 squares 2" x 2" (A)
Fabrics 3 and 4 – *cut from each:*
    2 squares 3¾" x 3¾" (B)

SEW

Sew together 2 each of the fabrics 1 and 2 squares to make a four-patch. Make 5. Use Trimming Guide A to trim each four-patch to size.

Draw a diagonal line on the wrong side of each fabric 3 or fabric 4 B square (whichever fabric is lighter). Place a fabric 3 and a fabric 4 B square right sides together with

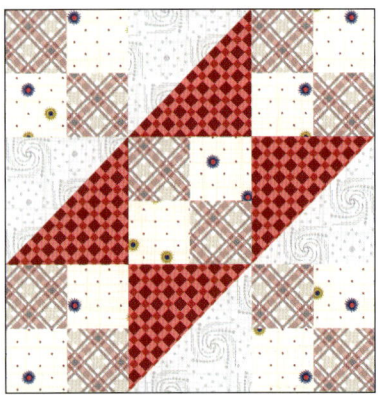

Jacob's Ladder
Color Options

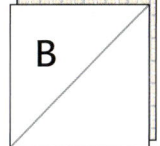 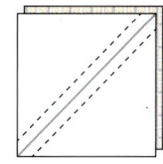 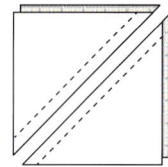 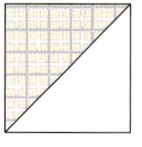 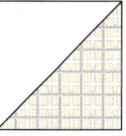

FROM THE PAGES OF
Lizzy Albright and the Attic Window, Chapter 11

There were five tiers of glass shelves and hundreds of ales, wines, and spirits from which to choose. Jacob, and some of the other shorter barmen, had to use a rolling ladder to reach the top two tiers where the most expensive libations were kept.

marked fabric on top. Sew 1/4" from each side of the marked line. Cut apart on the marked line to make 2 pieced squares. Repeat to make 4. Press seams towards the darker fabric. Use Trimming Guide B to trim each pieced square to size.

Sew 3 rows of 3 units each, watching fabric placement. Sew rows together to complete Jacob's Ladder block.

* = A trimmed
** = B trimmed

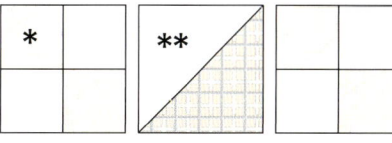
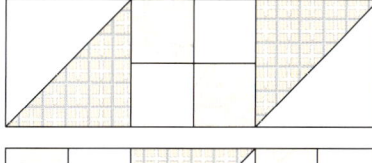

Jacob's Ladder Assembly

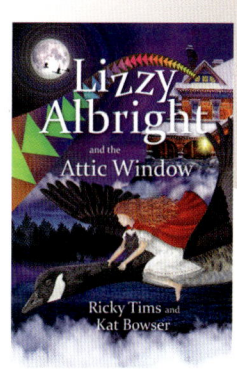

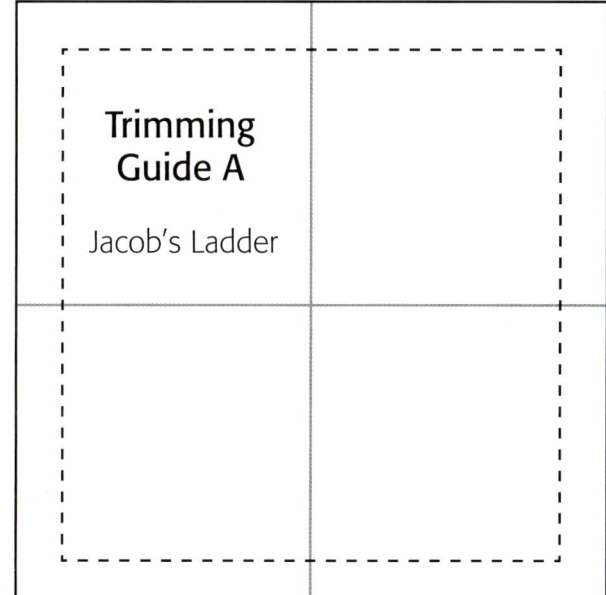

Trimming Guide A

Jacob's Ladder

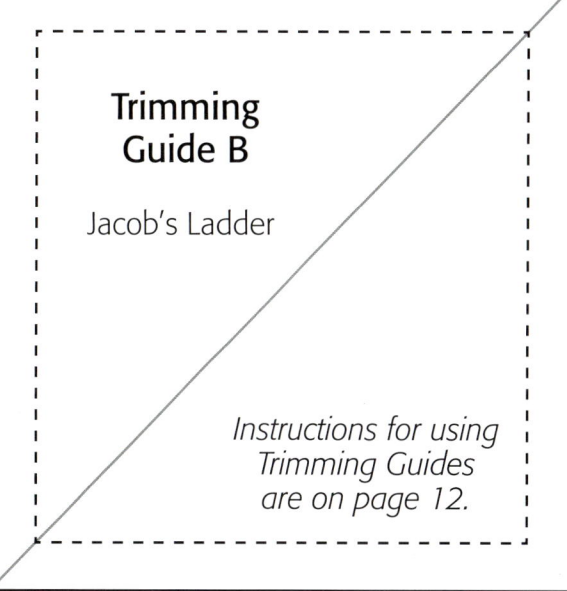

Trimming Guide B

Jacob's Ladder

Instructions for using Trimming Guides are on page 12.

Designed by Ricky Tims

5 Old Maid's Puzzle

The *Ladies Art Company* published a pattern for this block under the name Double X #3 as early as 1895, so this design is a true classic. Fox and Geese, School Girl's Puzzle, and Goose and Goslings are some of the other names given this quilt block.

FABRICS NEEDED

Fabric 1 (background): 10″ x 10″
Fabric 2 (2 small triangles): 3″ x 3″
Fabric 3 (large triangles and 4 small triangles): 8″ x 11″

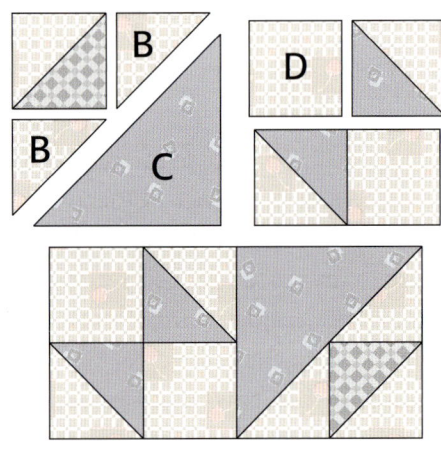

Old Maid's Puzzle
Assembly

Old Maid's Puzzle
Color Options

26 Granny's 1930 Sampler: From the Lizzy Albright Collection

CUT

Fabric 1
　3 squares 2⅞" x 2⅞" (A)
　2 squares 2⅞" x 2⅞" ◨ (B)
　4 squares 2½" x 2½" (D)

Fabric 2
　1 square 2⅞" x 2⅞" (A)

Fabric 3
　1 square 4⅞" x 4⅞" ◨ (C)
　2 squares 2⅞" x 2⅞" (A)

SEW

Use an accurate 1/4" seam allowance when piecing this block. Quarter-block units should measure 4½" square from raw edges to raw edges; if yours vary, adjust seam allowances until units are the correct size before assembling into rows and the block.

Draw a diagonal line on the wrong side of each fabric 1 A square. Place a fabric 1 and a fabric 2 A square right sides together with marked fabric on top. Sew 1/4" from each side of the marked line. Cut apart on the marked line to make 2 pieced squares. Press seams towards the darker fabric.

In the same way, use 2 fabric 1 and 2 fabric 3 A squares to make 4 pieced squares.

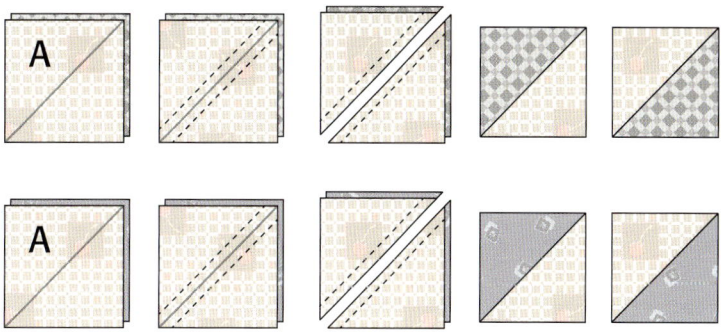

Stitch 2 fabric 1 B triangles to each fabric 1/fabric 2 pieced square. Add fabric 3 C triangle to make the upper left quarter-block. Repeat to make the lower right quarter-block.

Sew together 2 fabric 1 D squares and 2 fabric 1/fabric 3 pieced squares to make the upper right quarter-block. Repeat to make the lower left quarter-block.

Sew 2 rows of 2 quarter-blocks each. Sew rows together to complete the Old Maid's Puzzle block.

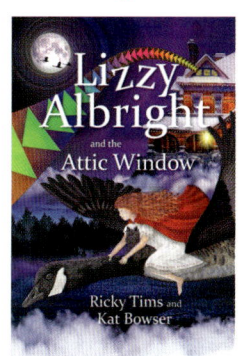

FROM THE PAGES OF
Lizzy Albright and the Attic Window, Chapter 6

Granny pointed out other blocks. "This is a Honey Bee block, and this one is called Old Maid's Puzzle." Lizzy giggled at that name but couldn't make out anything that resembled an old maid—or a puzzle.

Designed by Ricky Tims

6 Churn Dash

The well-known Churn Dash block is a simple variation of a nine-patch block. The blocks are seen in antique quilts dating back to the early 1800s. This simple design brings to mind the old-fashioned art of butter making. The pattern goes by many other names as well, including Monkey Wrench, Shoo Fly, Hole in the Barn Door, Lincoln's Platform, and Indian Hammer.

FABRICS NEEDED

Fabric 1 (churn dash): 8" x 9"
Fabric 2 (background): 9" x 12"

CUT

Fabric 1
   2 squares 3 3/4" x 3 3/4" (A)
   4 rectangles 2" x 3 1/4" (B)
Fabric 2
   2 squares 3 3/4" x 3 3/4" (A)
   4 rectangles 2" x 3 1/4" (B)
   1 square 3 1/4" x 3 1/4" (C)

Trimming Guide A

Churn Dash

Trimming Guide B

Churn Dash

Instructions for using Trimming Guides are on page 12.

28   Granny's 1930 Sampler: From the Lizzy Albright Collection

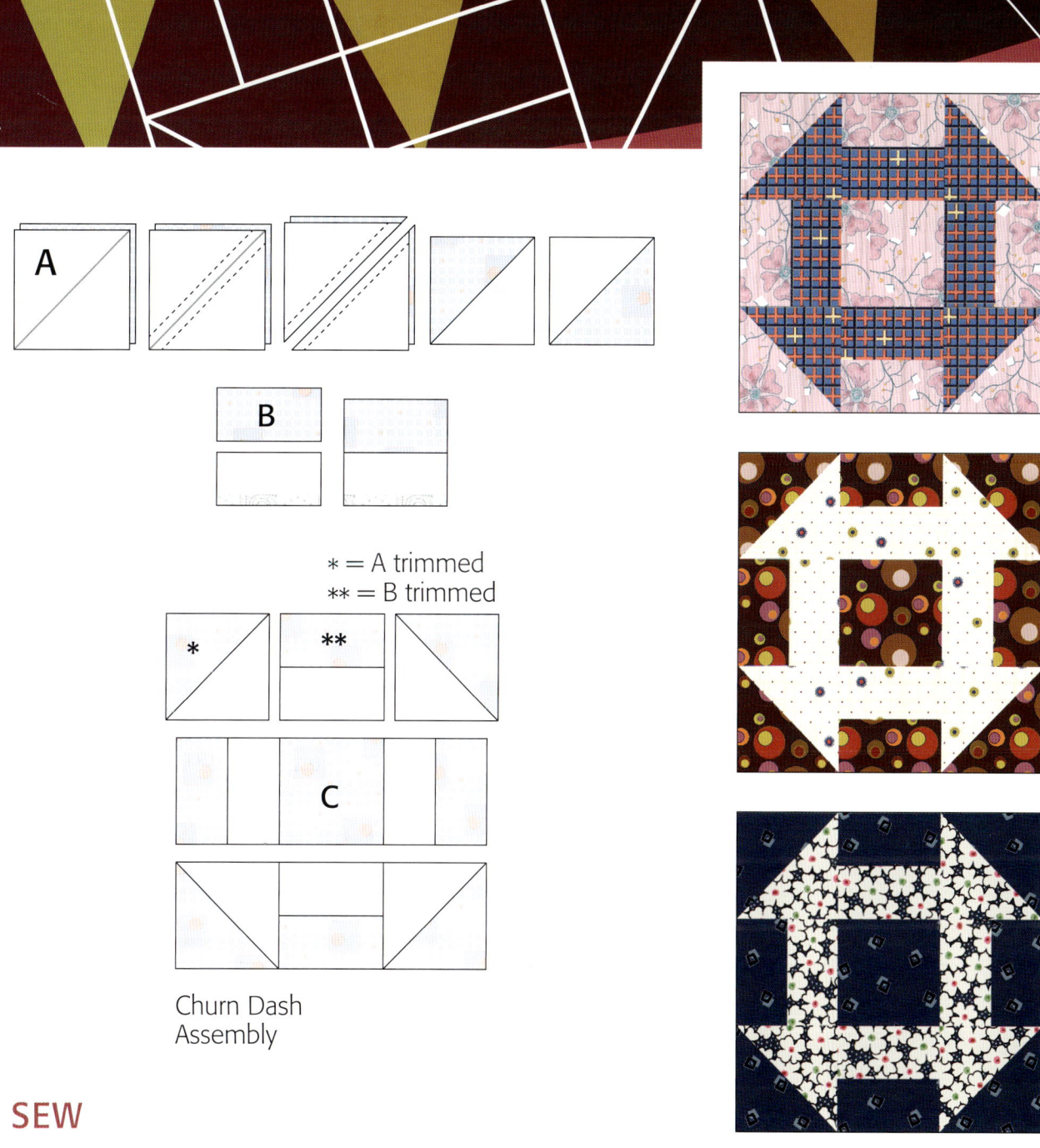

Churn Dash Assembly

Churn Dash Color Options

SEW

Draw a diagonal line on the wrong side of each fabric 1 A square. Place a fabric 1 and a fabric 2 A square right sides together with marked fabric on top. Sew 1/4" from each side of the marked line. Cut apart on the marked line to make 2 pieced squares. Make 4. Press seams towards the darker fabric. Use Trimming Guide A to trim each pieced square to size.

Sew together 1 each fabric 1 and fabric 2 B rectangles along long sides. Make 4. Press seams towards the darker fabric. Use Trimming Guide B to trim each unit to size.

Using either Trimming Guide, trim the Fabric 2 C square to size.

Sew 3 rows of 3 units each. Sew rows together to complete the Churn Dash block.

Designed by Ricky Tims

7 Storm at Sea

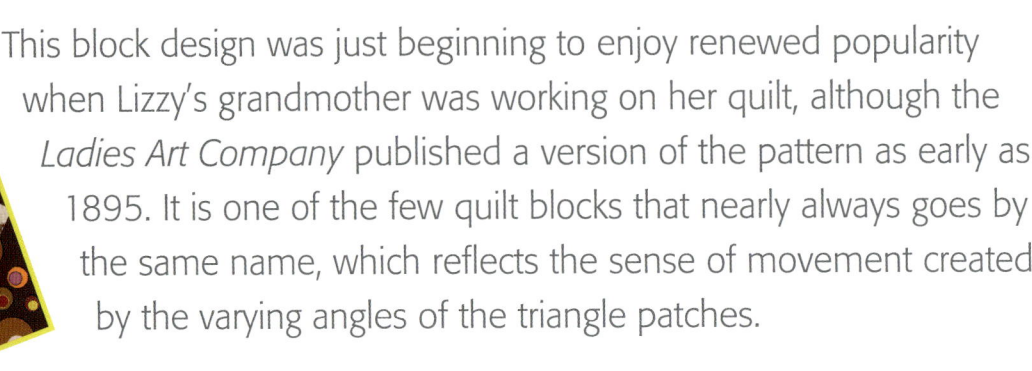

This block design was just beginning to enjoy renewed popularity when Lizzy's grandmother was working on her quilt, although the *Ladies Art Company* published a version of the pattern as early as 1895. It is one of the few quilt blocks that nearly always goes by the same name, which reflects the sense of movement created by the varying angles of the triangle patches.

FABRIC NEEDED

Fabric 1 (background): 12″ x 14″
Fabric 2 (units 1 and 3 corners): 9″ x 10″
Fabric 3 (unit 2 centers): 8″ x 8″
Fabric 4 (unit 3 center): 4″ x 4″

CUT

Fabric 1
  2 squares 3½″ x 3½″ ◨ (unit 3, areas 2 and 3)
  1 square 2¾″ x 2¾″ (unit 1, area 1)
  8 rectangles 2¼″ x 3½″ (unit 2, areas 2 and 3)
Fabric 2
  2 squares 4¼″ x 4¼″ ◨ (unit 3, areas 4 and 5)
  2 squares 3″ x 3″ ◨ (unit 1, areas 2 and 3)
Fabric 3
  2 rectangles 3½″ x 6¼″ (unit 2, area 1)
Fabric 4
  1 square 3½″ x 3½″ (unit 3, area 1)

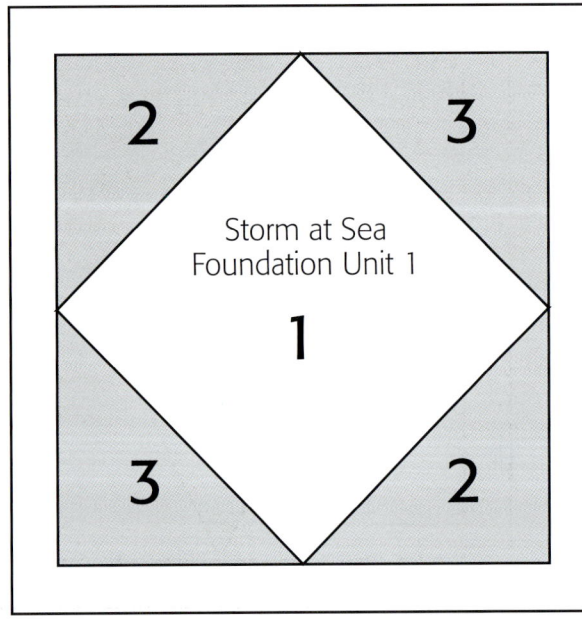

Instructions for foundation paper piecing are on page 14.

SEW

Make 1 accurate paper copy each of foundations 1 and 3, and 2 copies of foundation 2. Foundation piece 1 each of units 1 and 3, and 2 of unit 2. Trim edges even with outer lines on foundation papers.

Sew unit 1 and unit 2 together, matching lines on foundation papers, to make the top row of the block. Sew the remaining unit 2 and unit 3 together to make the bottom row. Sew rows together to complete the Storm at Sea block. Press well.

Sew a line of stay stitching inside the outer seam allowance of the block (about 1/8″ from the raw edges). Carefully remove all foundation paper from the back of the block.

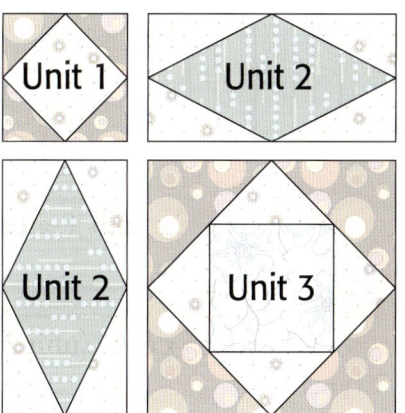

Storm at Sea Assembly

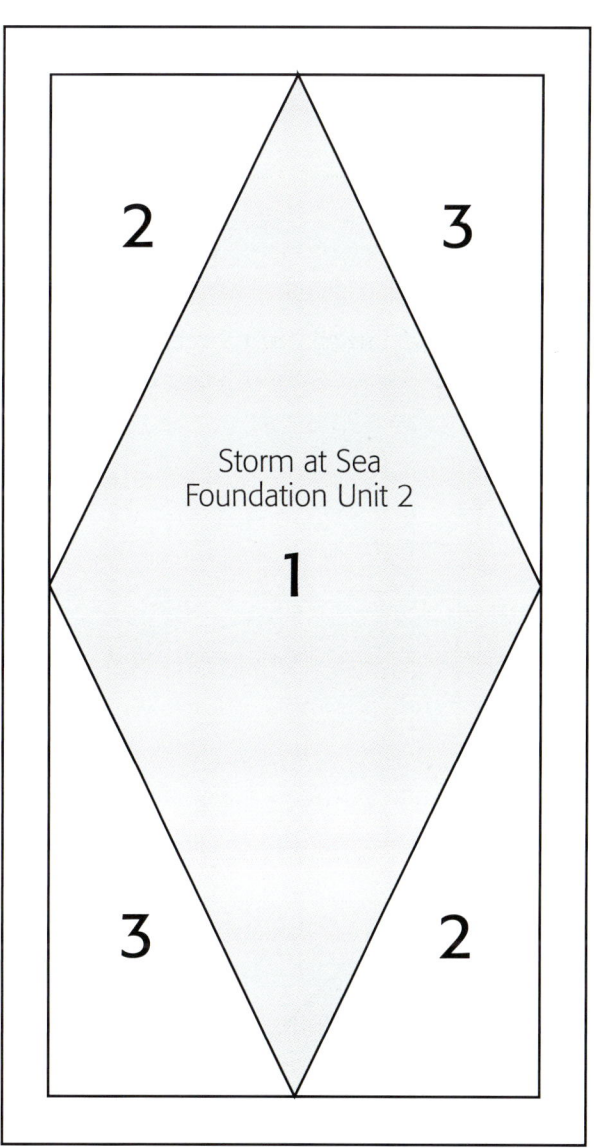

Designed by Ricky Tims

7 cont.

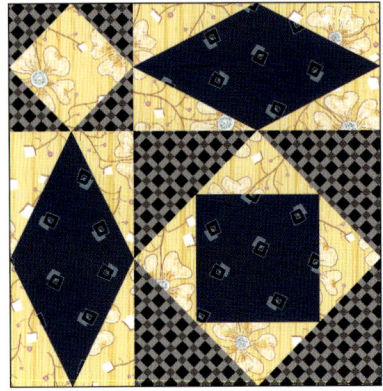

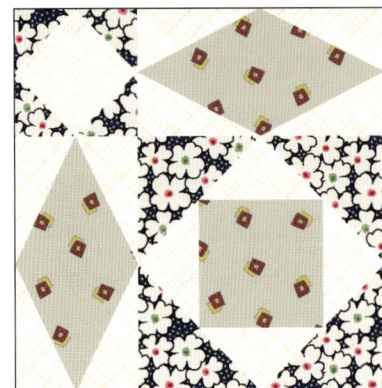

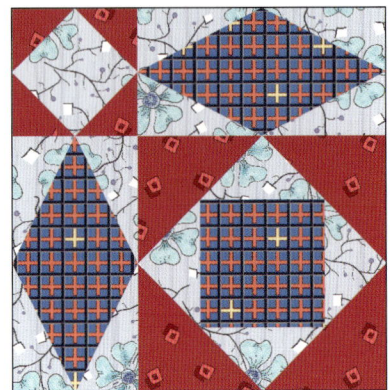

Storm at Sea
Color Options

Storm at Sea
Foundation Unit 3
1
2
2
3
3
4
4
5
5

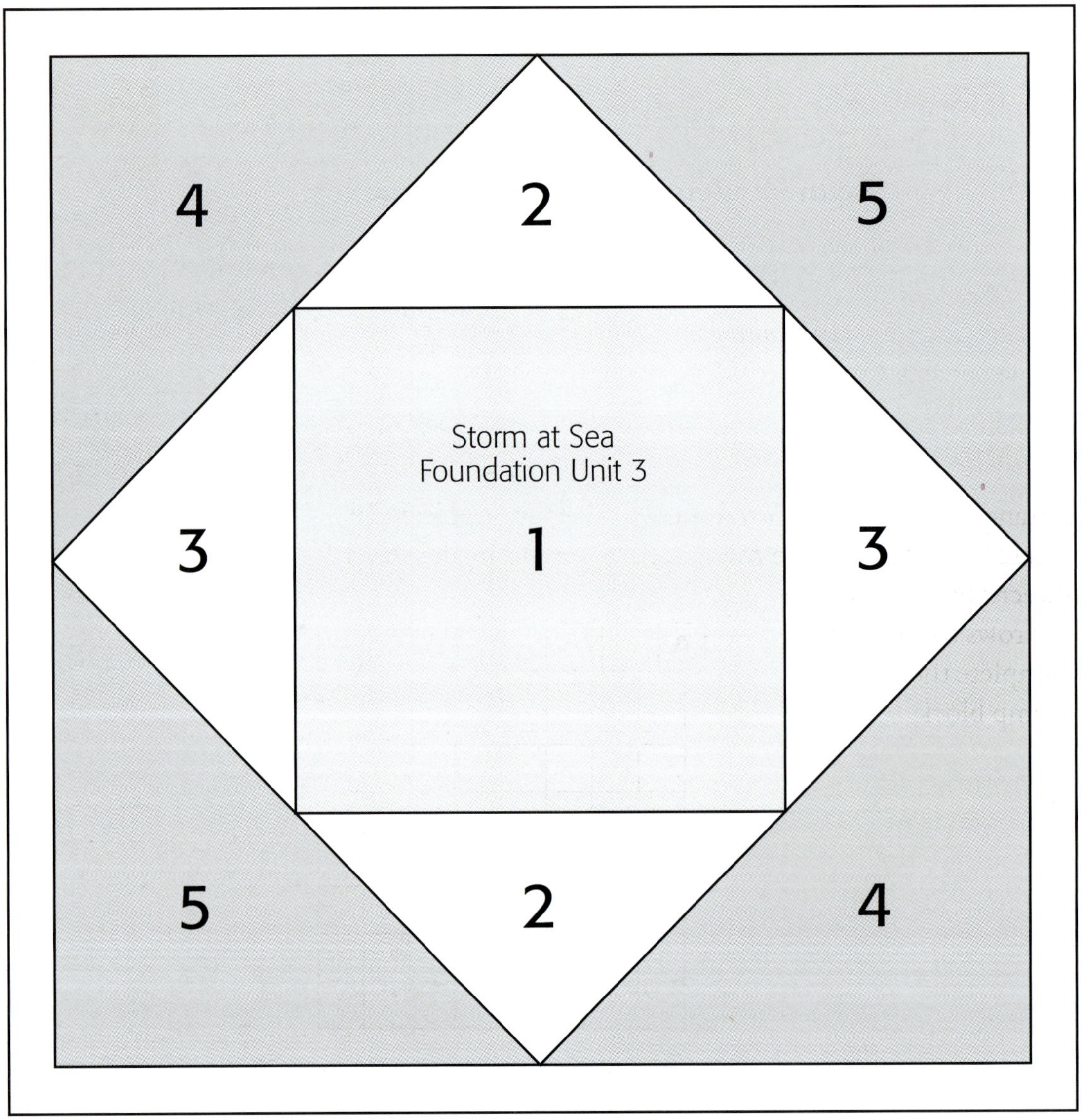

8 Postage Stamp

Lizzy's grandmother may well have made this block without any formal pattern, as it is simplicity itself. Published patterns for similar blocks date back at least to 1882. Here's a chance to mix up any fabrics you like…it's a great block for using small scraps.

Postage Stamp Color Options

FABRICS NEEDED

Fabric Group 1 (squares): assorted prints totaling ¼ yard

CUT

Fabric Group 1 – *cut a total of:*
64 squares 1½″ x 1½″ (A)

SEW

Arrange 8 rows of 8 assorted A each until fabric placement pleases you. Sew As into rows. Press the seams in alternate directions per row. Sew the rows together to complete the Postage Stamp block.

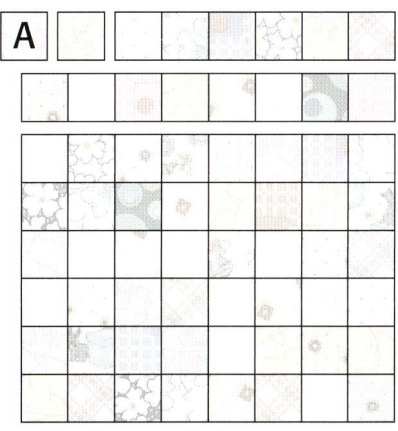

Postage Stamp Assembly

Designed by Ricky Tims

9 LeMoyne Star

Quilters do love their star blocks, and this particular design has appeared in published patterns at least as far back as 1899 in the *Orange Judd Farmer* magazine. The LeMoyne Star block is also sometimes called Twinkle Star, Eight-Pointed Star, or Star of the Milky Way.

FABRICS NEEDED

Fabric 1 (light): 14″ x 14″
Fabric 2 (dark): 14″ x 14″

CUT

Fabrics 1 and 2 – *cut from each:*
- 4 squares 3¼″ x 3¼″ (area 3)
- 4 rectangles 2½″ x 4¾″ (area 1)
- 4 squares 2½″ x 2½″ (area 2)

SEW

Make 4 accurate paper copies each of foundations 1 and 2. Foundation piece 4 each of units 1 and 2, paying attention to the orientation of any directional prints. Trim edges even with outer lines on foundation papers.

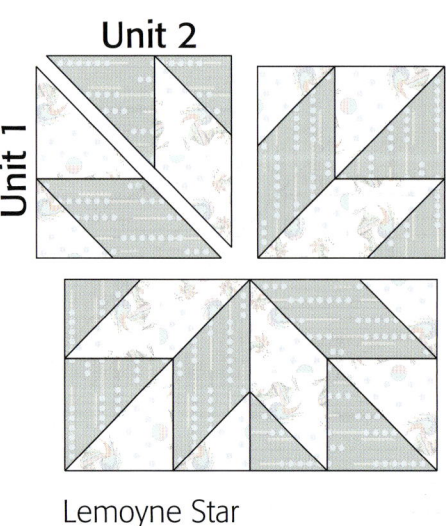

Lemoyne Star Assembly

Sew unit 1 and unit 2 together, matching lines on foundation papers, to make a pieced square. Make 4. Press seams open. Sew pieced squares together to complete the LeMoyne Star block, pressing seams open.

Sew a line of stay stitching inside the outer seam allowance of the block (about 1/8″ from the raw edges). Carefully remove all foundation paper from the back of the block.

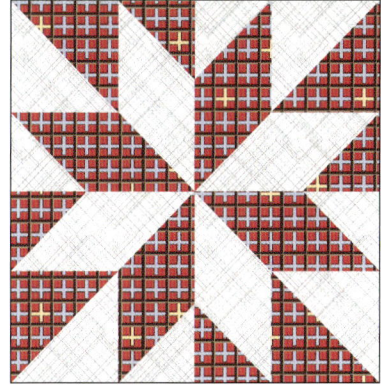

Lemoyne Star Color Options

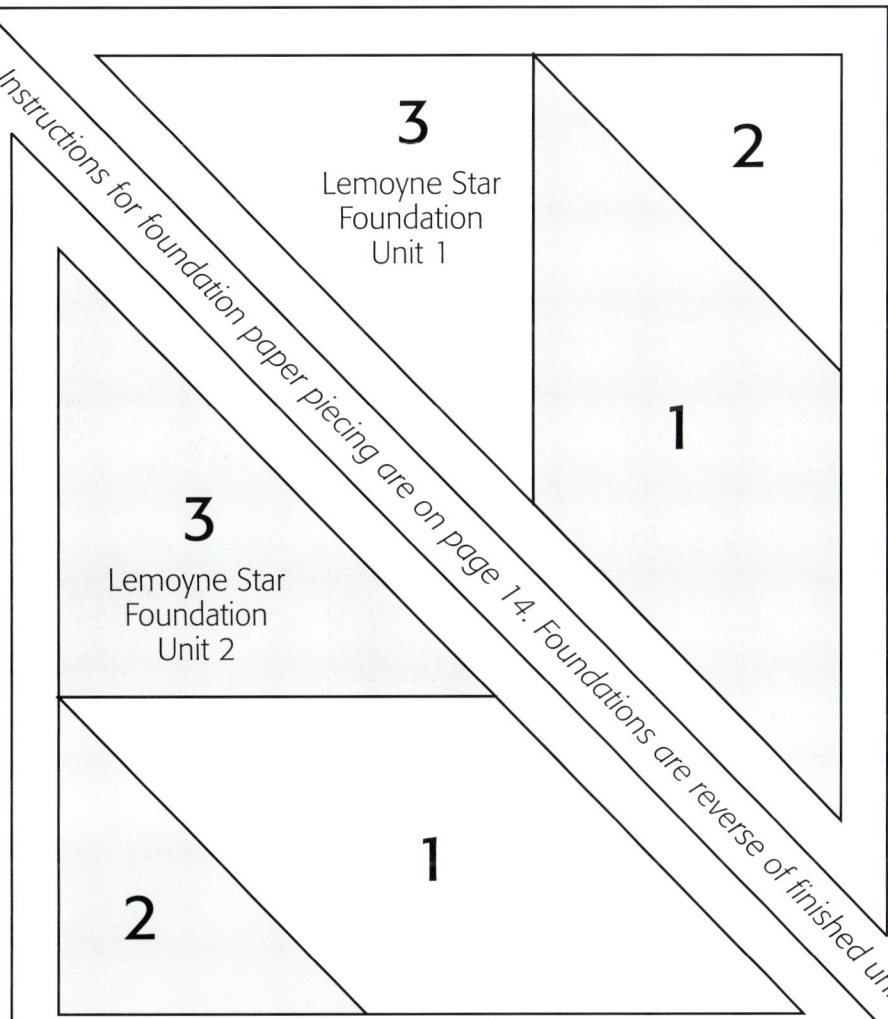

Designed by Ricky Tims

10 Snail's Trail

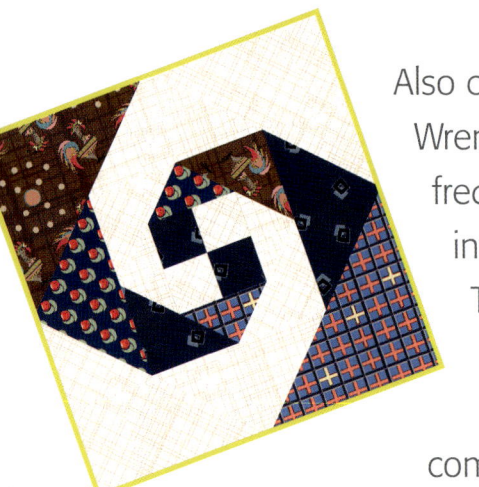

Also commonly called Monkey Wrench, Snail's Trail is the most frequent title used for this intriguing quilt block design. The optical illusion of curves gives it prime place as a focal block in Lizzy's complex quilt.

FABRICS NEEDED

Fabric 1 (background): 1 fat eighth (9" x 20-22" cut of fabric)
Fabric 2 (navy print in sample block): 6" x 8"
Fabric 3 (navy/red print in sample): 6" x 6"
Fabric 4 (blue plaid in sample): 7" x 8"
Fabric 5 (brown print in sample): 8" x 8"

CUT

Fabric 1
   2 rectangles 3¾" x 6½" (area 9)
   2 rectangles 2¾" x 4¾" (area 6)
   2 rectangles 2¼" x 3¾" (area 5)
   2 rectangles 1¾" x 2¾" (area 2)
   2 squares 1½" x 1½" (A for area 1 piecing)

Fabric 2
   1 rectangle 2¾" x 4¾" (area 7)
   1 rectangle 2¼" x 3¾" (area 4)
   2 squares 1½" x 1½" (A for area 1 piecing)

Fabric 3
   1 rectangle 2¾" x 4¾" (area 7)
   1 rectangle 1¾" x 2¾" (area 3)

Fabric 4
   1 rectangle 3¾" x 6½" (area 8)
   1 rectangle 1¾" x 2¾" (area 3)

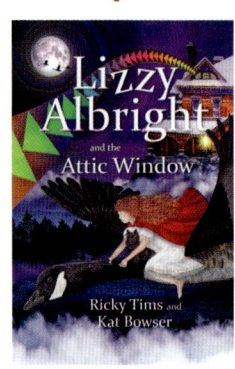

FROM THE PAGES OF
Lizzy Albright and the Attic Window, Chapter 12

Miona waved them over. She had managed to snag a bistro table near the back corner of the Snail's Trail. Sitting on the table was a pitcher of rummyritas and two extra glasses that had sat waiting patiently for them to arrive. The atmosphere at the Snail's Trail was always cozy and comfortable.

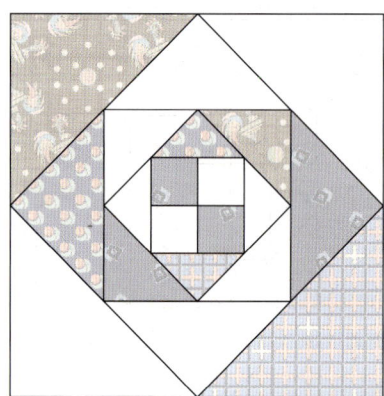

Snail's Trail Assembly

Granny's 1930 Sampler: From the Lizzy Albright Collection

Fabric 5
  1 rectangle 3¾" x 6½" (area 8)
  1 rectangle 2¼" x 3¾" (area 4)

SEW

Sew fabrics 1 and 2 A squares together to make a four-patch, pressing seams open. Four-patch should measure 2½" square from raw edge to raw edge.

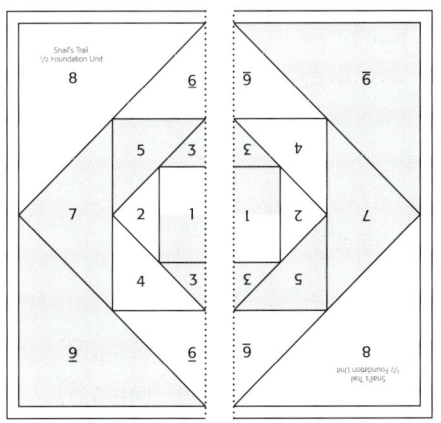

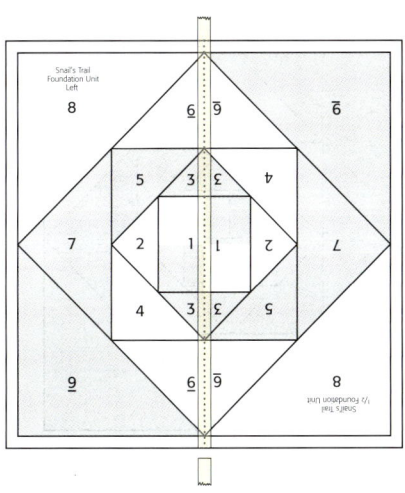

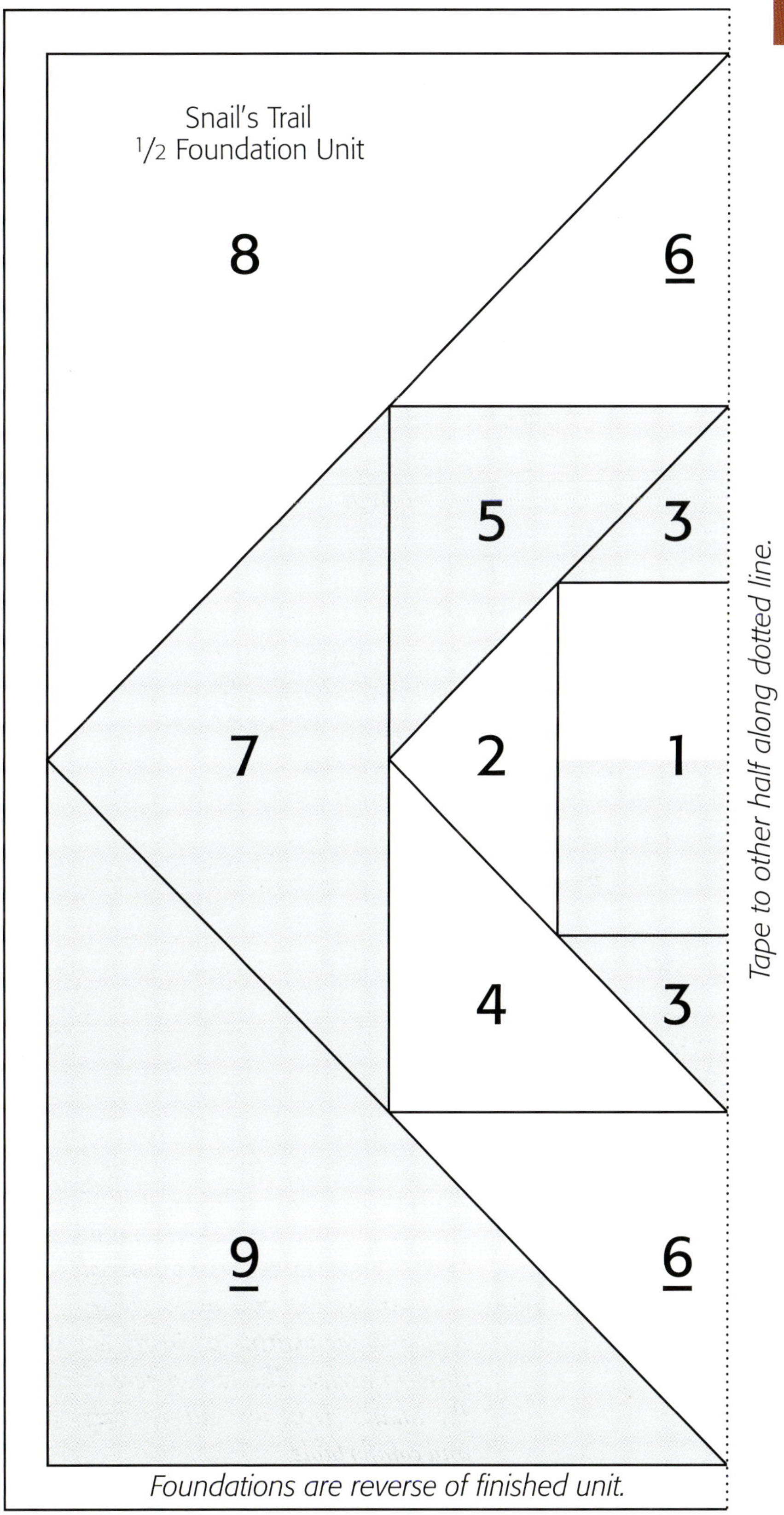

Designed by Ricky Tims

10 cont.

  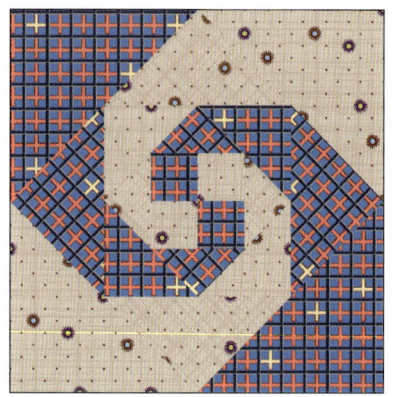

Snail's Trail
Color Options

Make an accurate paper copy of the foundation (tape copies of half-foundations together as shown). Place the foundation on a light box or tape it to a window or other light source with the *unprinted* side facing you.

Use a glue stick to adhere the *wrong* side of the four-patch to the *unprinted* side of the foundation on area 1.

Foundation piece the remainder of the block, treating the four-patch as area 1. Trim edges even with outer lines on foundation paper.

Sew a line of stay stitching inside the outer seam allowance of the block (about 1/8" from the raw edges). Carefully remove all foundation paper from the back of the block.

Instructions for foundation paper piecing are on page 14.

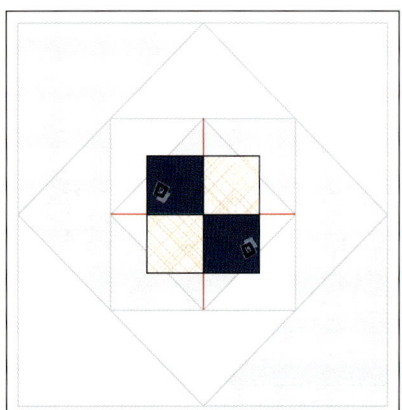 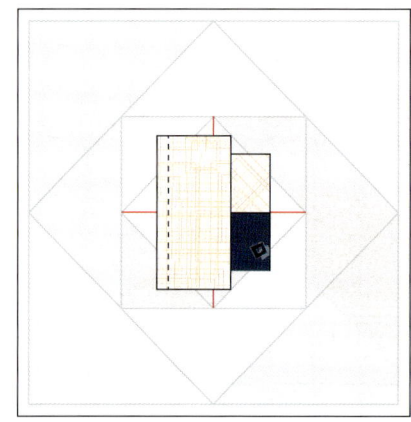 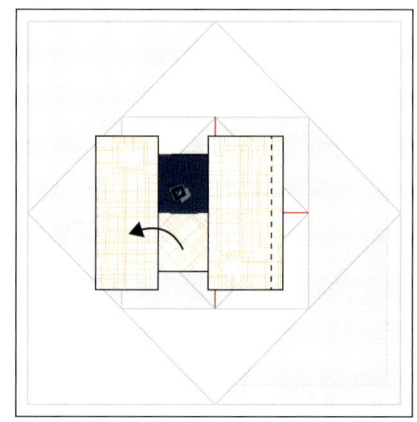

Unprinted side of foundation.

38 Granny's 1930 Sampler: From the Lizzy Albright Collection

11 Double Pinwheel

Also known as Turnstile, Windmill, Whirlwind, and Whirligig, this block design has a great sense of depth and movement. Published patterns for this quilt block date back at least as far as 1904.

Double Pinwheel Assembly

FABRICS NEEDED

Fabric 1 (background): 6″ x 6″
Fabric 2 (center triangles): 6″ x 6″
Fabric 3 (large triangles): 5″ x 10″

CUT

Fabrics 1 and 2 – *cut from each*:
　1 square 5¼″ x 5¼″ ⊠ (A)
Fabric 3
　2 squares 4⅞″ x 4⅞″ ◻ (B)

SEW

Sew 1 each of fabric 1 and fabric 2 A triangles together to make a pieced triangle. Make 4.

Stitch a fabric 3 B triangle to pieced triangle to make a quarter-block. Make 4.

Watching orientation, sew 2 rows using the 4 quarter-blocks. Sew the rows together to complete the Double Pinwheel block.

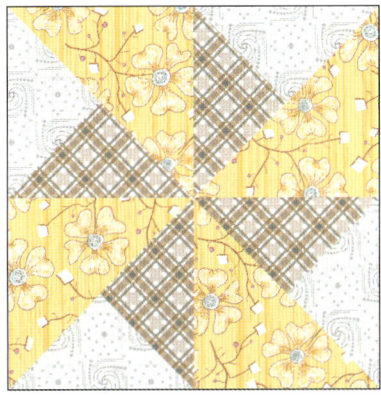

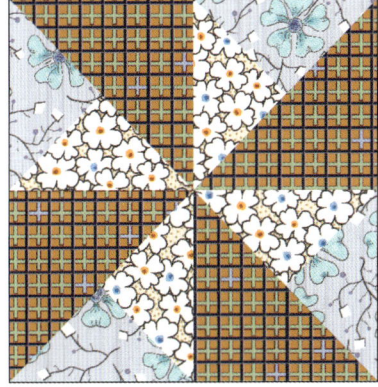

Double Pinwheel Color Options

Designed by Ricky Tims

12 Square in a Square

This simple quilt block goes by many names, including Economy or Economy Patch, Hour Glass, Thrift Block, and This and That. It became very popular in the years leading up to the Great Depression, and is still enjoyed by quilters today, especially as a way to feature fussy-cut fabric motifs in a center square. Lizzy's grandmother showed off a colorful print in her center patch.

Square in a Square Assembly

FABRICS NEEDED

Fabric 1 (center): 5" x 5"
Fabric 2 (center triangles): 6" x 11"
Fabric 3 (corner triangles): 7" x 14"

CUT

Fabric 1
    1 square 4 3/4" x 4 3/4" (area 1)
Fabric 2
    2 squares 4 1/2" x 4 1/2" ◻ (areas 2 and 3)
Fabric 3
    2 squares 5 3/4" x 5 3/4" ◻ (areas 3 and 4)

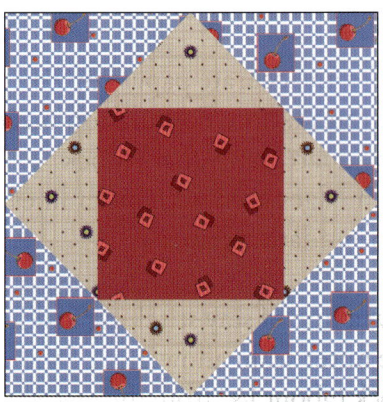

Square in a Square Color Options

Granny's 1930 Sampler: From the Lizzy Albright Collection

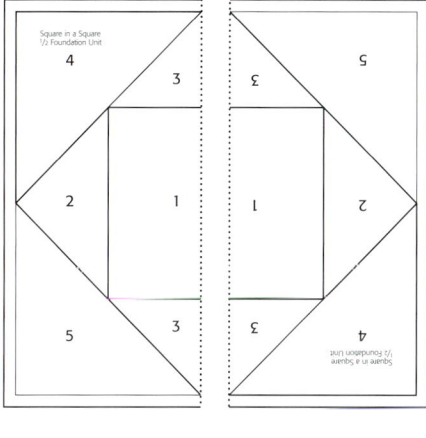

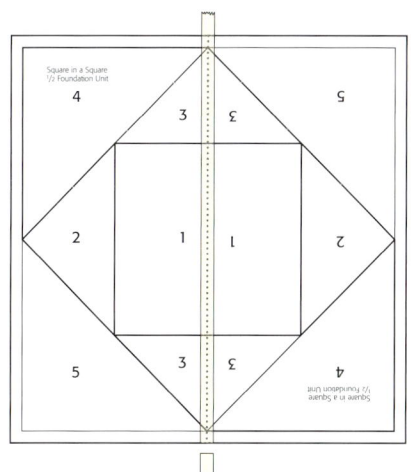

SEW

Make an accurate paper copy of the foundation. Foundation piece the Square in a Square block. Trim edges even with outer lines on foundation paper.

Sew a line of stay stitching inside the outer seam allowance of the block (about 1/8" from the raw edges). Carefully remove all foundation paper from the back of the block.

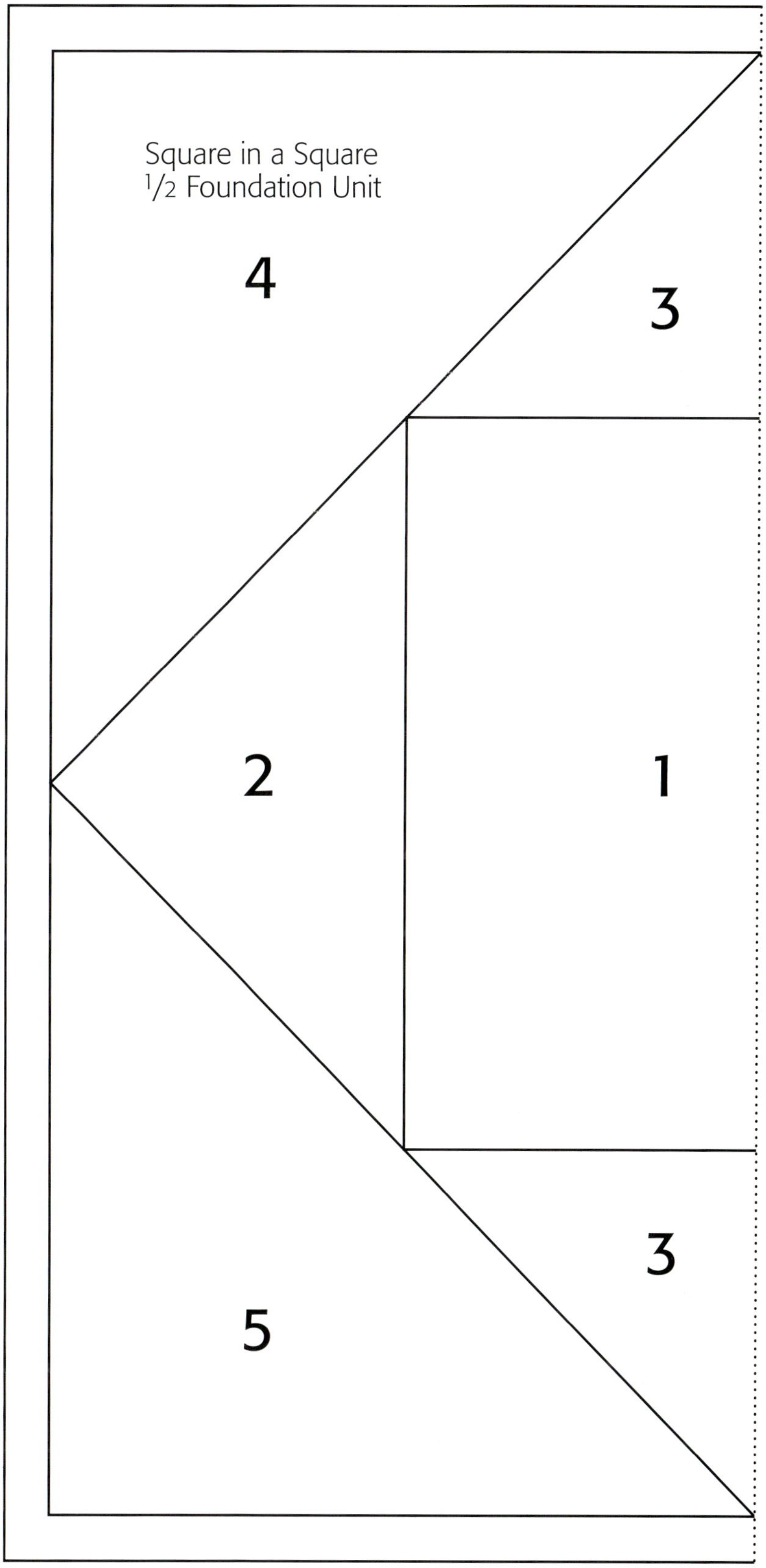

Square in a Square
1/2 Foundation Unit

Instructions for foundation paper piecing are on page 14. Tape to other half along dotted line.

Designed by Ricky Tims

13 Robbing Peter to Pay Paul

Although the origin of the phrase from which this quilt block gets its name dates as far back as the time of King Edward VI in the mid-1500s, the design itself is not quite so old! Quilters of the 1920s and 30s loved this block for its graphic impact, requiring just one dark and one light fabric to achieve. Other names associated with this design include Orange Peel, Dolly Madison's Workbox, Love Ring, and Sugar Bowl.

FABRICS NEEDED

Fabric 1 (dark): 12″ x 14″
Fabric 2 (light): 12″ x 14″

CUT

Fabrics 1 and 2 – *cut from each*:
  2 Template A
  8 Template B

SEW

Stitch fabric 2 B patches to opposite sides of a fabric 1 A patch, aligning dots. Add fabric 2 B patches to remaining sides to complete a quarter-block. Make 2 of this fabric arrangement. Trim to 4½″ x 4½″ if needed.

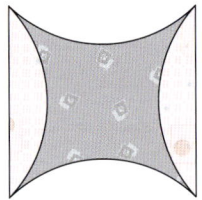 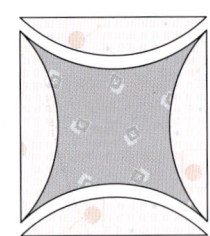

In the same way, make 2 quarter-blocks of the reversed fabric arrangement (fabric 1 B patches sewn to fabric 2 A patch).

Sew 2 rows of 2 quarter-blocks each. Sew rows together to complete the Robbing Peter to Pay Paul block.

FROM THE PAGES OF
Lizzy Albright and the Attic Window, Chapter 6

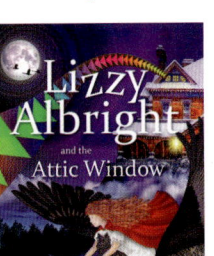

Lizzy woke up but didn't open her eyes. She pulled the covers up under her chin and felt the softness of the quilt. She was still wondering who robbed Peter to pay Paul and whether one of the bees in the Honey Bee block was a queen bee.

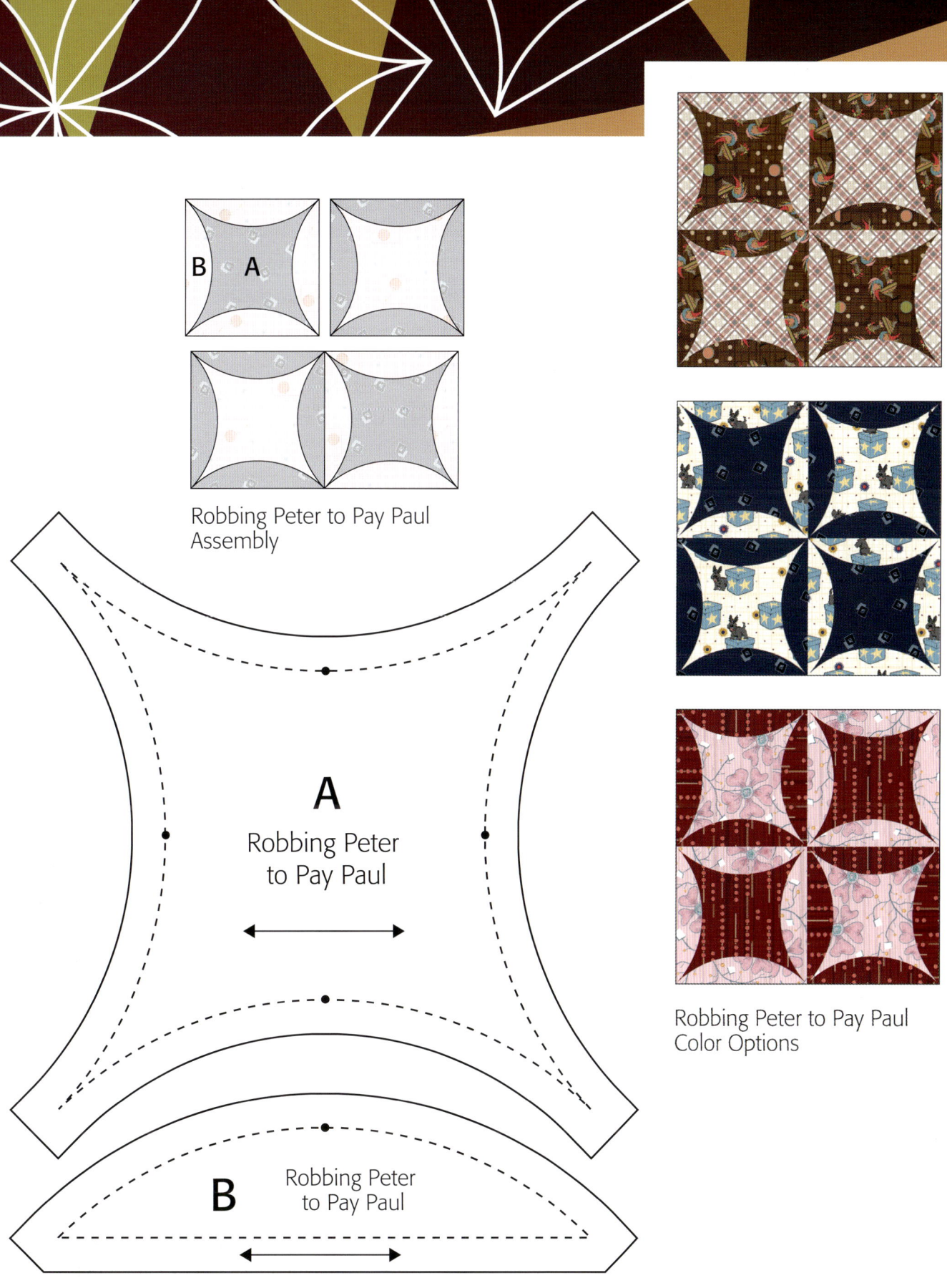

Robbing Peter to Pay Paul Assembly

A
Robbing Peter to Pay Paul

B
Robbing Peter to Pay Paul

Robbing Peter to Pay Paul Color Options

Designed by Ricky Tims 43

14 Scottie Dog

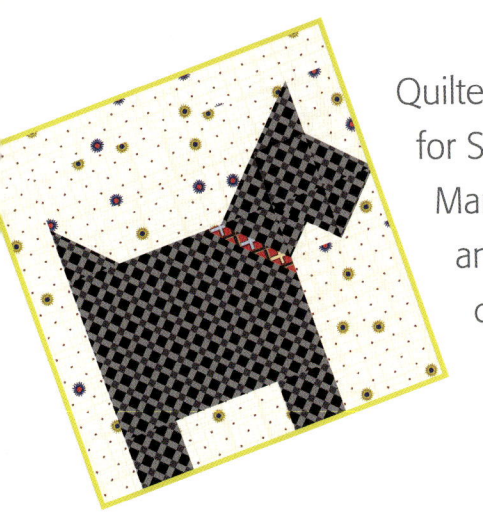

Quilters in the years following World War I had a lot of affection for Scottie dogs if their quilts and other crafts are any indication. Many stuffed dogs were made with simple fabric squares, and the basic dog design appeared in lots of versions of this delightful block.

FABRICS NEEDED

Fabric 1 (background): 10″ x 12″
Fabric 2 (dog): 9″ x 12″
Fabric 3 (collar): 1″ x 4″

CUT

Fabric 1
    1 *each* Templates A, C, D, and G
    5 Template B
    2 Template F
    1 strip 1½″ x 7½″ (H)
    1 strip 1½″ x 8½″ (I)
Fabric 2
    1 *each* Templates A and E
    6 Template B
    3 Template C
Fabric 3
    1 optional collar

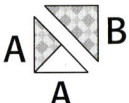

Chin square.

Make 5.

SEW

Sew together the fabric 1 and fabric 2 A triangles. Add a fabric 2 B triangle to make the chin pieced square.

Sew together 1 each fabric 1 and fabric 2 B triangles to make a triangle square. Make 5.

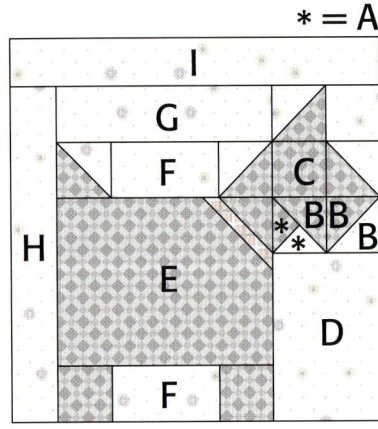

Scottie Dog Assembly

Sew 3 rows using 3 triangle squares, 1 each fabric 1 and fabric 2 C squares, and the chin pieced square. Sew rows together to make the dog head. Stitch D to bottom of dog head.

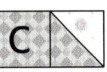
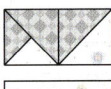

Head section.

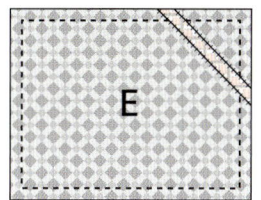

Add optional collar.

Collar: Press under ¼" on long edges of collar shape, trimming seam allowances a bit if needed to reduce bulk. Pin or glue-baste the prepared shape to E, aligning raw edges. Appliqué long edges of collar to E. The short edges of the collar will be caught in the seams.

Sew triangle squares to ends of F to make pieced strip for dog's back. Sew fabric 2 Cs to ends of remaining F to make pieced strip for dog's legs. Stitch G, pieced strip for dog's back, E, and pieced strip for dog's legs together to make dog body.

Sew dog body and dog head sections together to make the dog.

Sew H to left side of dog. Sew I to top to complete Scottie Dog block.

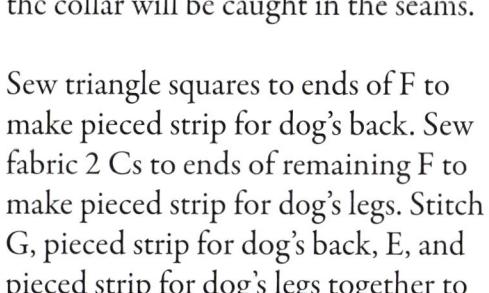

Body section.

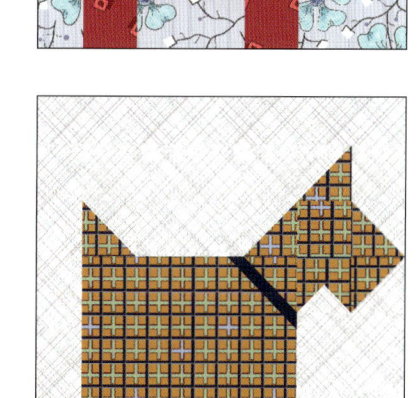

Join sections.

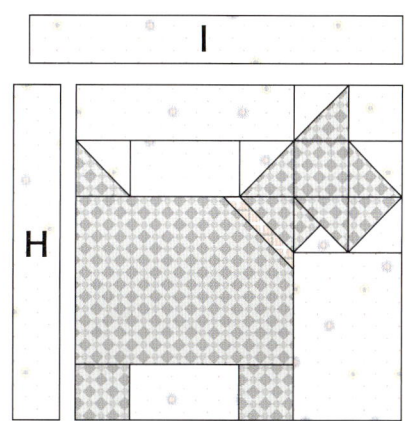

Scottie Dog Color Options

Designed by Ricky Tims

14 cont.

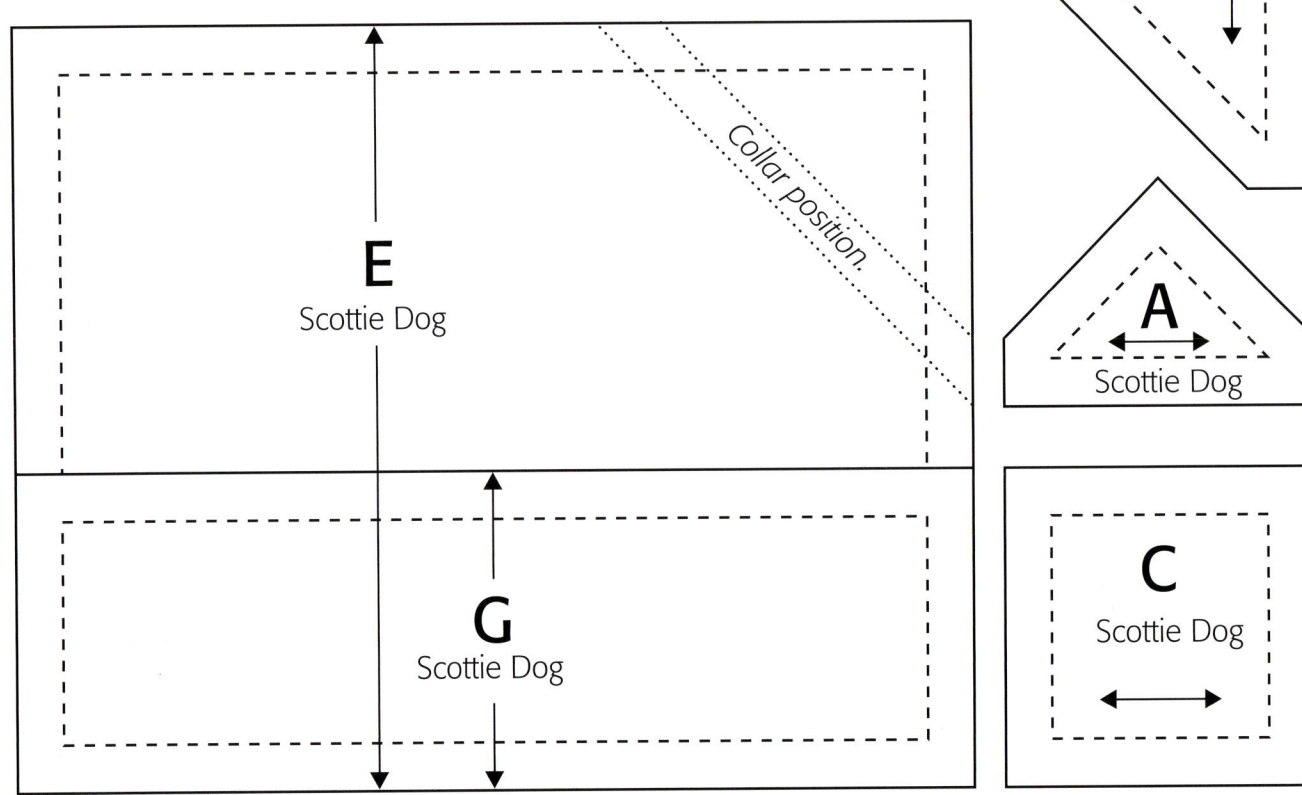

FROM THE PAGES OF
Lizzy Albright and the Attic Window, Chapter 6

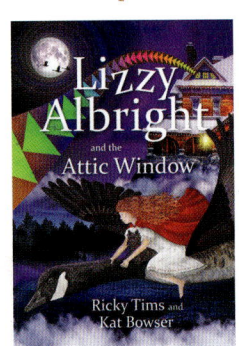

"I remember that block, Mom. It always reminded me of Toshie."

"Who was Toshie?" asked Lizzy.

"When I was your age, we had a Scottie named Toshie. Toshie was short for Macintosh. He was notorious for chasing the geese away from the pond outside. Remember that, Mom?"

"Oh Lord, yes, I remember. He would race after those geese and they would scatter to the four winds like marbles dropped on a dance floor. He then pranced back to the house as if he had just saved his castle from an invasion of winged water rats. Those poor geese!"

Granny's 1930 Sampler: From the Lizzy Albright Collection

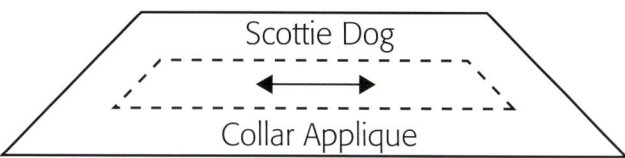

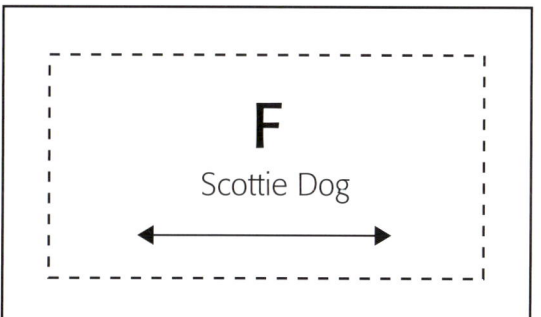

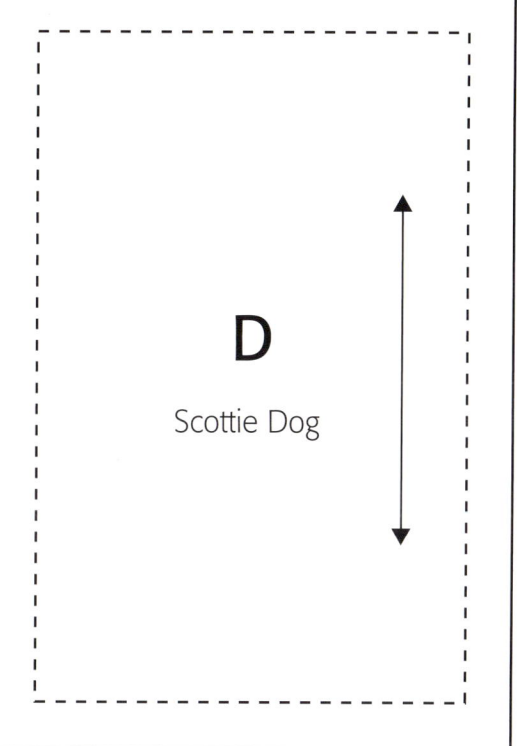

Chapter 7

"It's a pleasure to meet you too, Mr. McDoogle."

"But I do need to tell ye..." said McDoogle.

"What's that?" asked Gretta.

"I'll be keepin' a beady eye on ye. I won't be allowin' ony tomfoolery."

"Alright, Mr. McDoogle. Alright! No tomfoolery."

Designed by Ricky Tims

15 Double Nine-Patch

Marie Webster published a pattern for this block as early as 1915, so Lizzy's grandmother would have had access to instructions if she needed them. This block is sometimes also referred to as Single Irish Chain, since the blocks when set together create that beloved design.

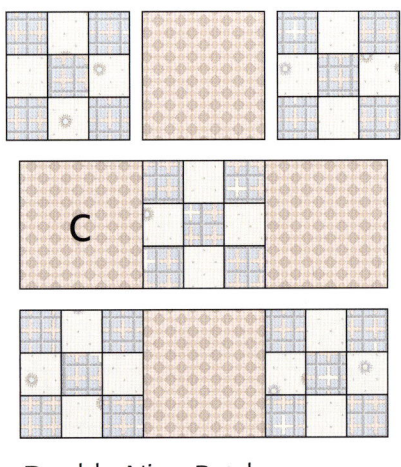

Double Nine Patch Assembly

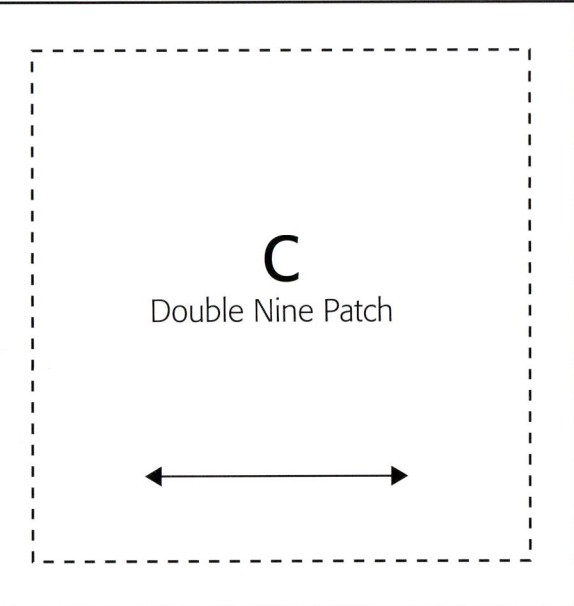

C
Double Nine Patch

Double Nine Patch Color Options

48 Granny's 1930 Sampler: From the Lizzy Albright Collection

FABRICS NEEDED

Fabric 1 (dark): 6″ x 17″
Fabric 2 (light): 6″ x 17″
Fabric 3 (background): 8″ x 8″

CUT

Fabric 1
  *2 strips 1½″ x 16″ (A)
  *1 strip 1½″ x 9″ (B)

Fabric 2
  *1 strip 1½″ x 16″ (A)
  *2 strips 1½″ x 9″ (B)

Fabric 3
  4 Template C

*After cutting strips as listed, trim to exact width using the Trimming Guide.

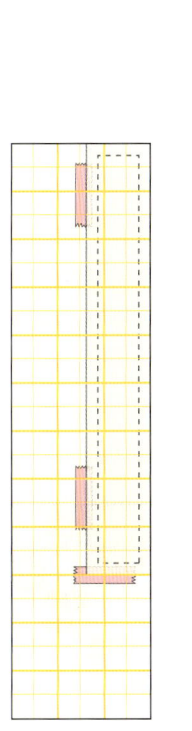

Align trimming template with ruler corner and tape to back of ruler.

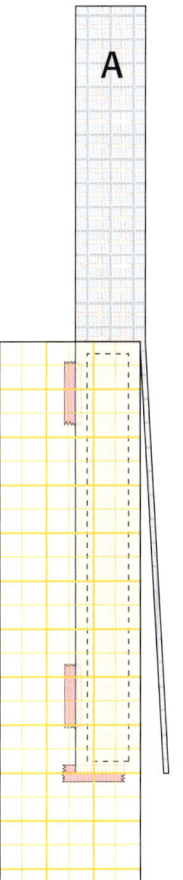

Align left edge of template with left edge of rough-cut strip. Trim.

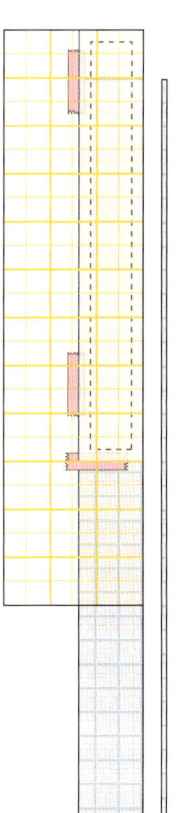

Realign left edge of ruler with upper strip and finish the trim.

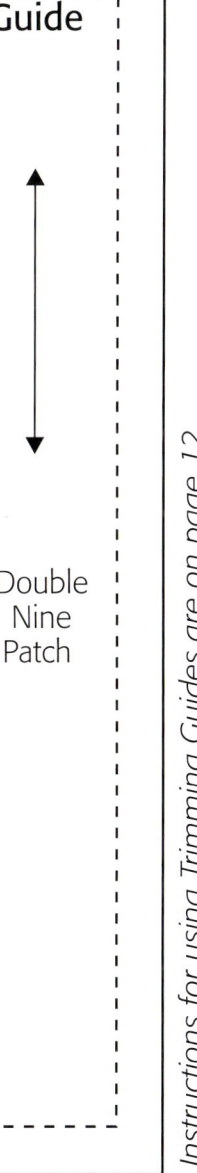

Trimming Guide

Double Nine Patch

Instructions for using Trimming Guides are on page 12.

Designed by Ricky Tims

15 cont.

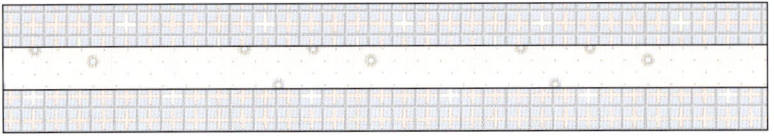

A Pieced Strip

B Pieced Strip

SEW

Stitch the 3 trimmed A strips together on their long sides, alternating fabrics; press well. Do the same with the 3 trimmed B strips. From the longer pieced strip, cut 10 segments using the Trimming Guide for the exact width; you will have extra left over. From the shorter pieced strip, cut 5 segments in the same way.

Sew together 3 segments to make a nine-patch. Make 5.

Sew 3 rows using the 5 nine-patches and 4 Cs. Sew the rows together to complete the Double Nine-Patch block.

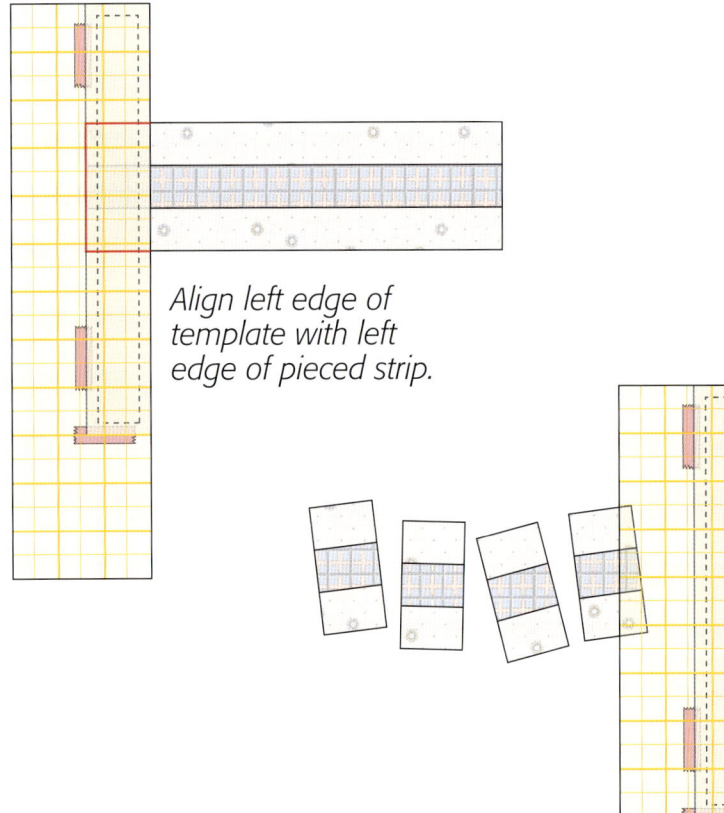

Align left edge of template with left edge of pieced strip.

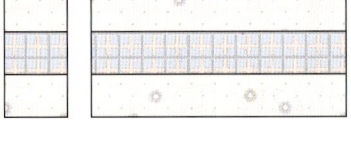

Cut segments.

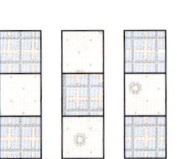

Join segments.   *Make 5.*

50   Granny's 1930 Sampler: From the Lizzy Albright Collection

16 Sawtooth Star

An early version of this block pattern was published by *Farm and Fireside* magazine in 1884. A much-loved classic, it also goes by many other names, including Evening Star, Cluster of Stars, Austin, Optical Sawtooth, and Square and Points.

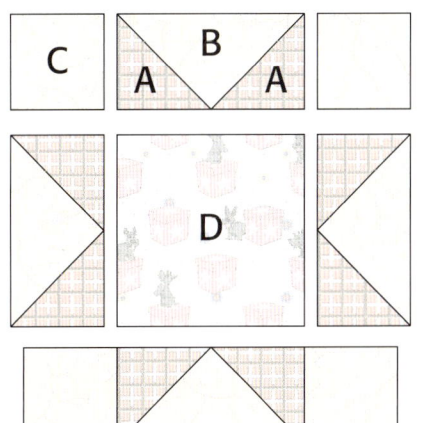

Sawtooth Star Assembly

FABRICS NEEDED

Fabric 1 (points): 6″ x 6″
Fabric 2 (background): 8″ x 8″
Fabric 3 (center): 5″ x 5″

CUT

Fabric 1
 4 squares 2 7/8″ x 2 7/8″ ◻ (A)
Fabric 2
 1 square 5 1/4″ x 5 1/4″ ⊠ (B)
 4 squares 2 1/2″ x 2 1/2″ (C)
Fabric 3
 1 square 4 1/2″ x 4 1/2″ (D)

SEW

Sew fabric A triangles to sides of fabric B triangle to make a star point unit. Make 4.

Sew 3 rows using 4 fabric 2 C squares, 4 star point units, and fabric 3 D square. Sew rows together to complete the Sawtooth Star block.

Sawtooth Star Color Options

Designed by Ricky Tims

17 New York Beauty

This old quilt block design has gone by names as diverse as Chinese Fan, Flo's Fan, Crown of Thorns, and Rocky Mountain Road, but it became popular as New York Beauty in the 1920s thanks to the Stearns and Foster Company. They included patterns for the design in packages of Mountain Mist cotton batting during that era, and the rest is New York Beauty history!

FABRICS NEEDED

Fabric 1 (arc background): 10″ x 12″
Fabric Group 2 (points): assorted prints totaling 8″ x 10″
Fabric 3 (corner arc): 5″ x 5″
Fabric 4 (narrow arc): 6″ x 6″
Fabric 5 (background): 9″ x 9″

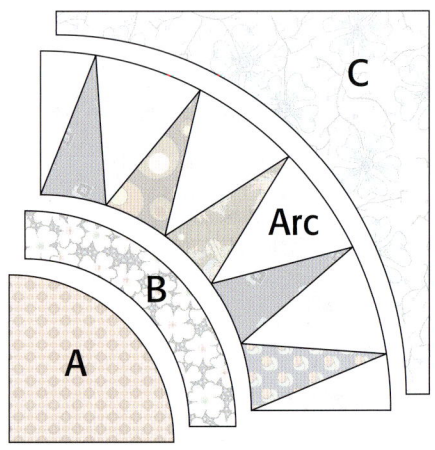

New York Beauty Assembly

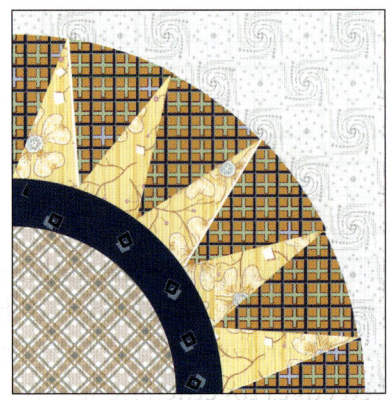

New York Beauty Color Options

52 Granny's 1930 Sampler: From the Lizzy Albright Collection

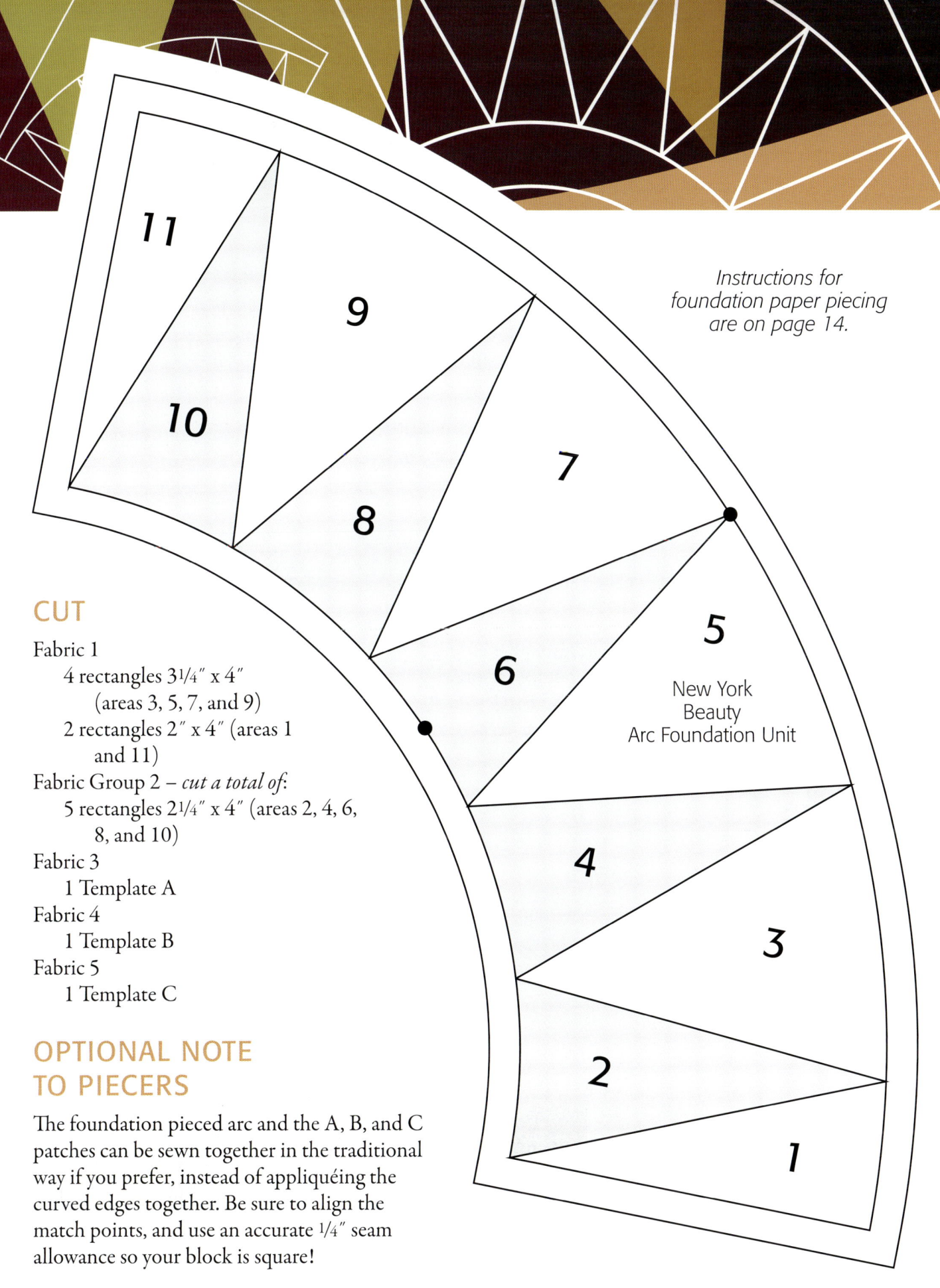

Instructions for foundation paper piecing are on page 14.

New York Beauty
Arc Foundation Unit

CUT

Fabric 1
 4 rectangles 3¼" x 4" (areas 3, 5, 7, and 9)
 2 rectangles 2" x 4" (areas 1 and 11)

Fabric Group 2 – *cut a total of*:
 5 rectangles 2¼" x 4" (areas 2, 4, 6, 8, and 10)

Fabric 3
 1 Template A

Fabric 4
 1 Template B

Fabric 5
 1 Template C

OPTIONAL NOTE TO PIECERS

The foundation pieced arc and the A, B, and C patches can be sewn together in the traditional way if you prefer, instead of appliquéing the curved edges together. Be sure to align the match points, and use an accurate ¼" seam allowance so your block is square!

Designed by Ricky Tims

17 cont.

SEW

Make an accurate paper copy of the arc foundation. Foundation piece the arc. Trim edges even with outer lines on the foundation paper. Sew a line of stay stitching inside the outer seam allowance (about 1/8″ from the raw edges). Carefully remove the foundation paper from the back of the arc.

To make pressing guides, trace B and C shapes *without seam allowances on the curved edges* onto heat-resistant template plastic, light card stock, or a stack of 3 sheets of freezer paper pressed together. Cut out the B and C guides on the traced lines.

Place the C pressing guide on the wrong side of the C patch, aligning the straight raw edges, and use spray starch and an iron to press under the curved edge 1/4″. You will need to

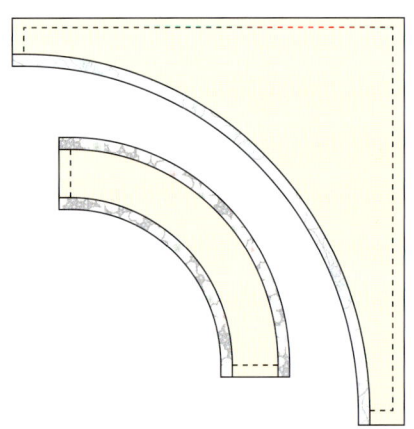

Wrong side.

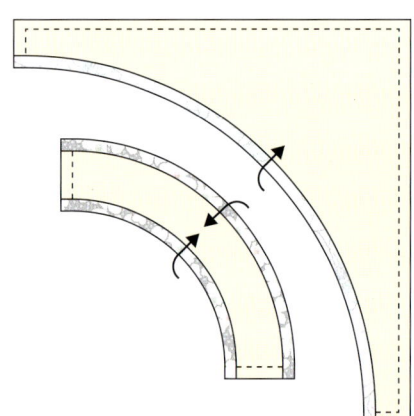

Spray and press.

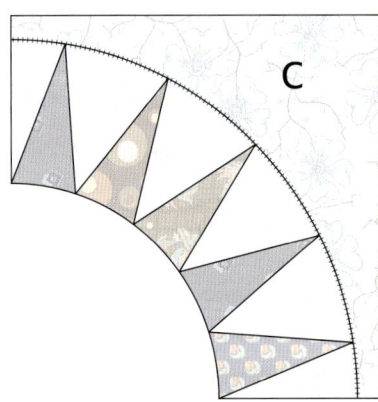

Appliqué curved edge of C to arc.

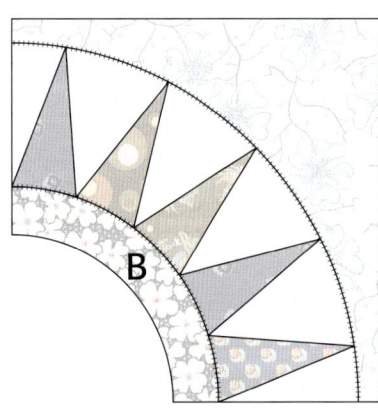

Appliqué curved edge of B to arc.

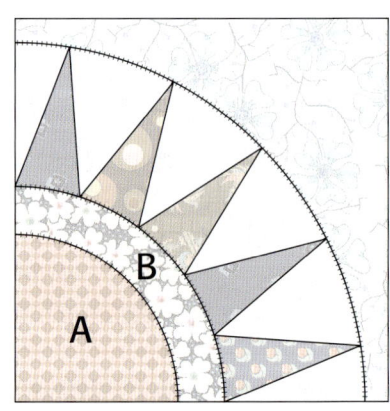

Appliqué remaining curved edge of B to A.

54 Granny's 1930 Sampler: From the Lizzy Albright Collection

clip the curved edge of the fabric to make a smooth curve. Pin or glue-baste the prepared C shape to the larger curve of the arc, aligning the pressed edge with the points on the arc. Appliqué the curved edge in place.

In the same way, prepare, pin or glue-baste, and appliqué the larger curve of B to the smaller curve of the arc, and the smaller curve of B to the curved edge of A to complete the New York Beauty block.

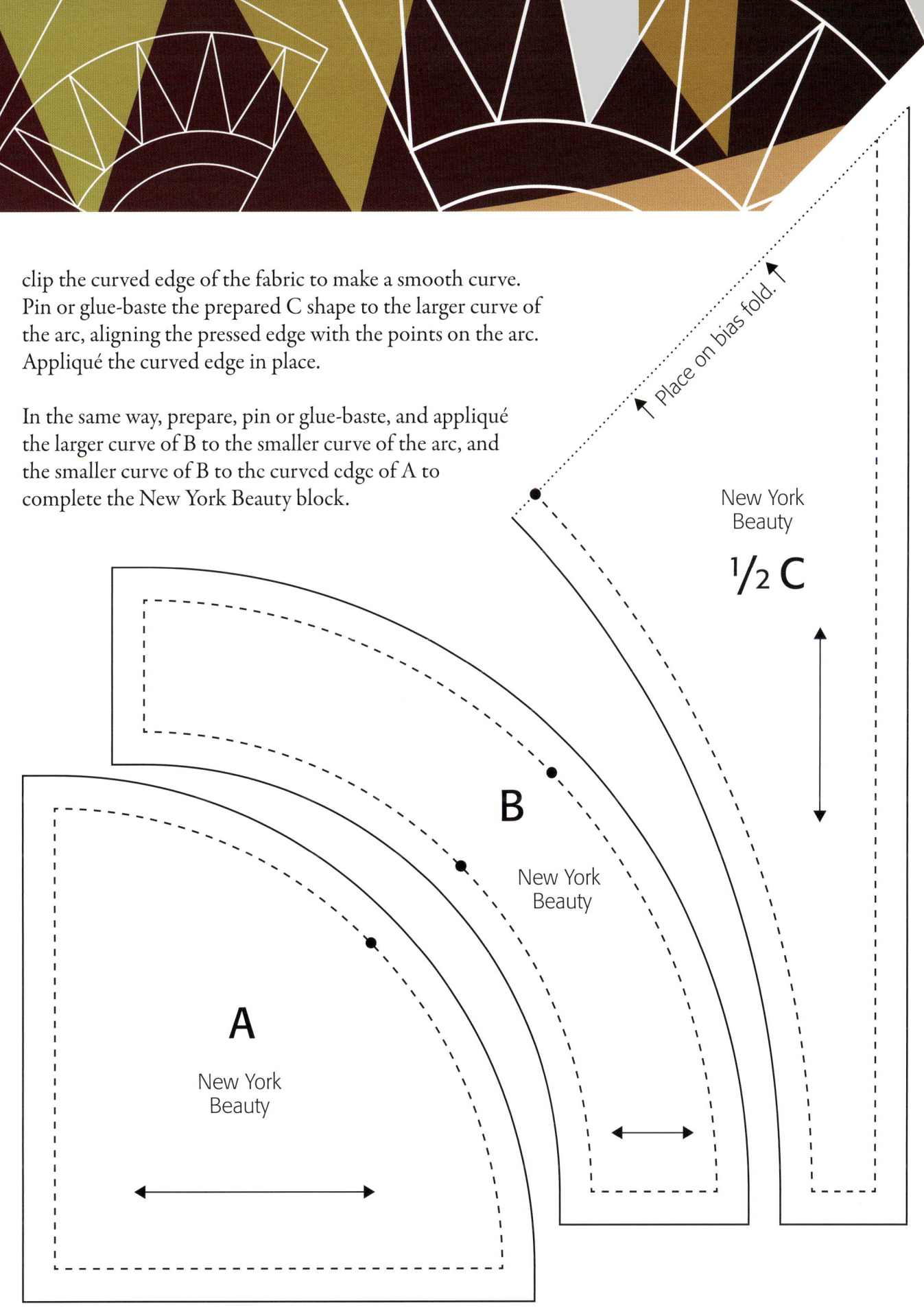

Designed by Ricky Tims

18 Ohio Star

This is one of those quilt blocks with so many common names that it's hard to keep track of them all, but it's commonly recognized as Ohio Star by today's quilters. Its distinguishing feature is the quarter-square triangle units used to make the 8 star points. The Ohio Star design dates back to the early 1800s, and enjoyed a surge of popularity in the 1920s through 1930s.

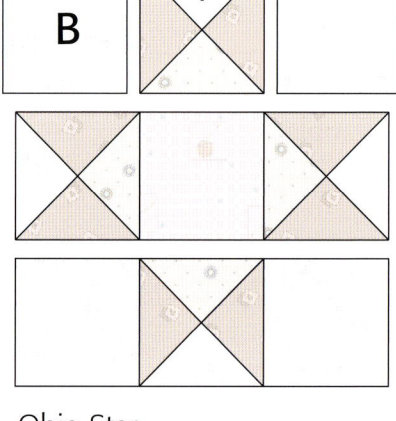

Ohio Star Assembly

∗ = A trimmed

FABRICS NEEDED

Fabric 1 (background): 7″ x 12″
Fabric 2 (star points): 5″ x 9″
Fabric 3 (center triangles): 5″ x 5″
Fabric 4 (center square): 4″ x 4″

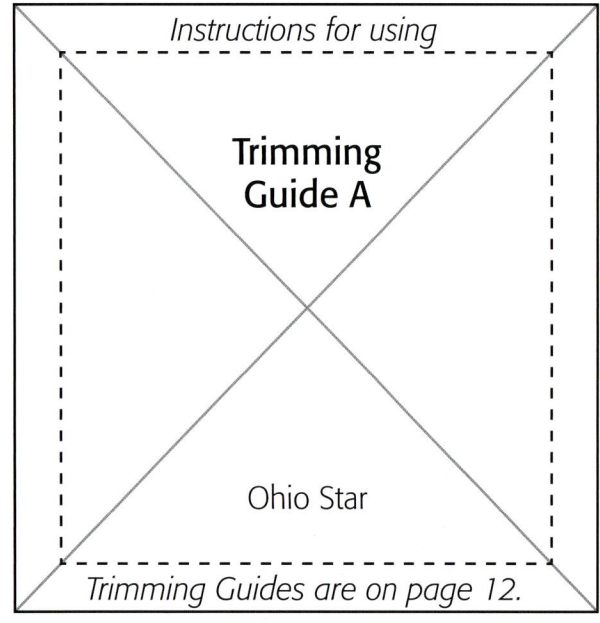

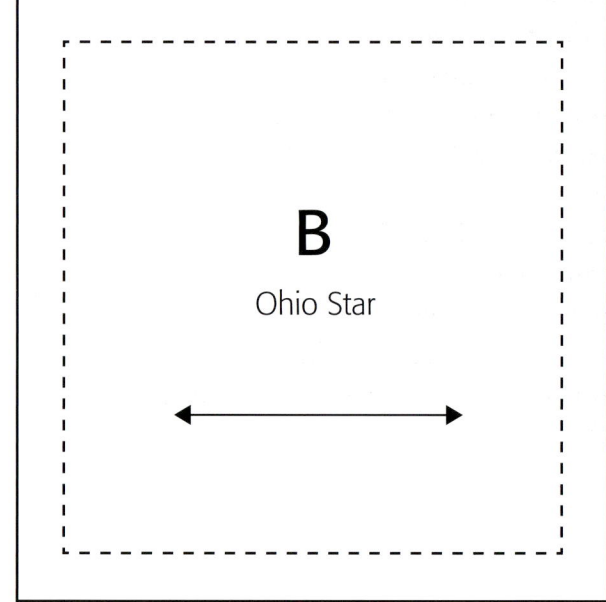

Trimming Guides are on page 12.

56   Granny's 1930 Sampler: From the Lizzy Albright Collection

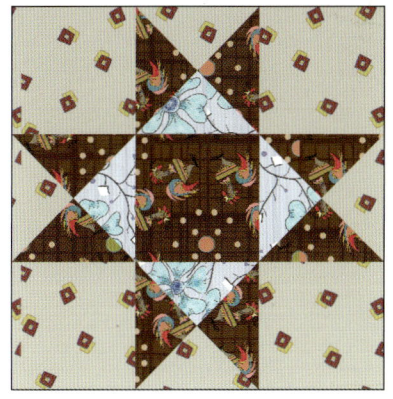

Ohio Star
Color Options

CUT

Fabric 1
    1 square 4″ x 4″ (A)
    4 Template B

Fabric 2
    2 squares 4″ x 4″ (A)

Fabric 3
    1 square 4″ x 4″ (A)

Fabric 4
    1 Template B

SEW

Draw 2 diagonal lines on the wrong side of each fabric 2 A square. Place a marked square on the fabric 1 A square, right sides together. Sew ¼″ seam on each side of one line. Cutting on the unsewn line first, then on the remaining drawn line, cut sewn square into quarters. Press open to make pieced triangles. Use second marked fabric 2 A square and the fabric 3 A square to make 4 pieced triangles in the same way.

Sew 2 pieced triangles together to make a star point unit, watching fabric placement carefully. Make 4 star point units. Use the Trimming Guide to trim to exact size, aligning seams with gray lines on the Guide.

Sew 3 rows using 4 fabric 1 Bs, 4 trimmed star point units, and 1 fabric 4 B. Sew the rows together to complete the Ohio Star block.

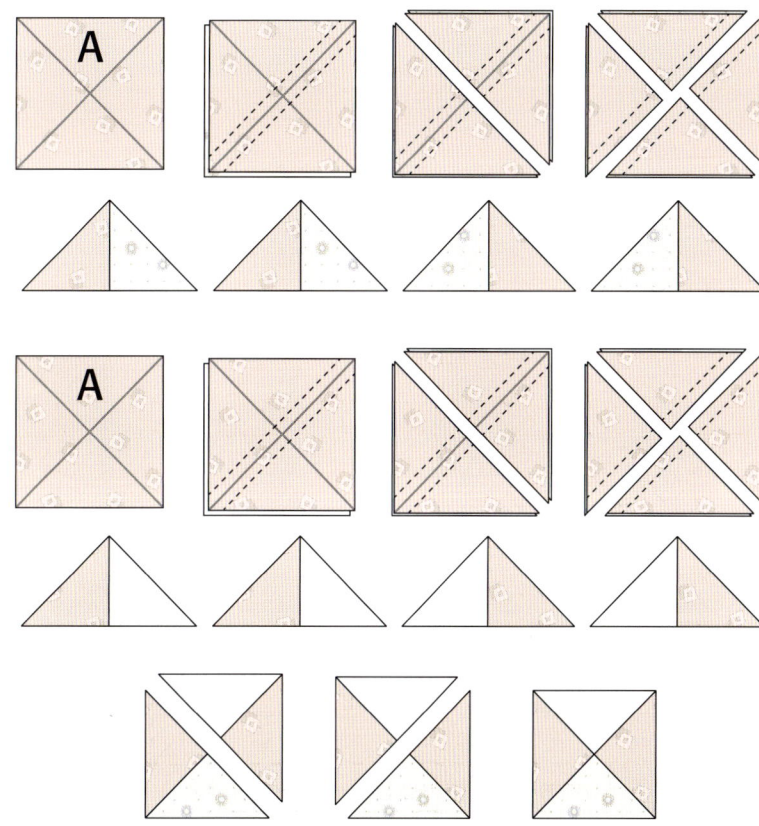

Designed by Ricky Tims

19 Rail Fence

One of the simplest of all quilt blocks, the Rail Fence is also variously known as Fence Post, Roman Square, Roman Stripe, and Fine Woven. Depending on fabric placement and block orientation, quilts made of multiples of this block can take on a zigzag pattern and lots of other variations.

FABRICS NEEDED

Fabrics 1, 2, 3, and 4: 2″ x 20″ *each*

CUT

Fabrics 1, 2, 3, and 4 – *cut from each:*
1 strip 1½″ x 20″

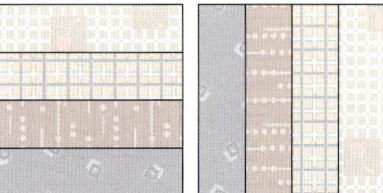

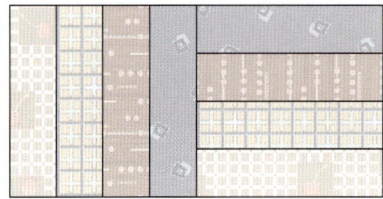

Rail Fence Assembly

  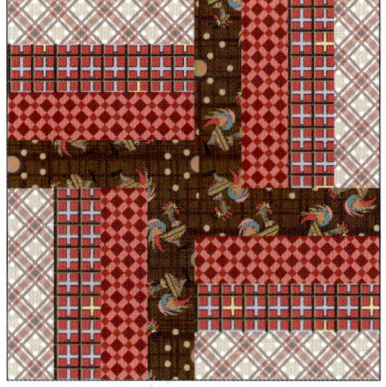

Rail Fence Color Options

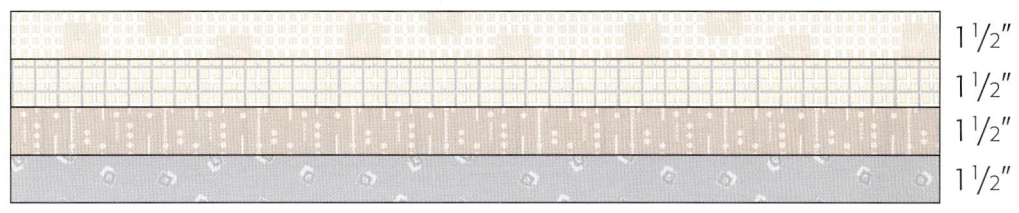

1½"
1½"
1½"
1½"

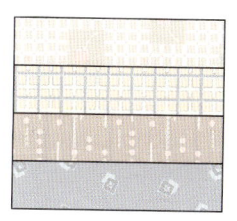 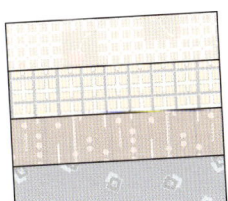 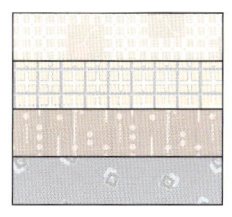 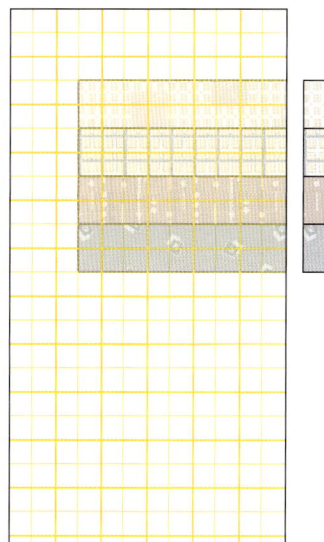

4½"

SEW

Sew fabric 1, 2, 3, and 4 strips together along long sides; press well. From the strip set, cut 4 segments each 4½" wide.

Sew 2 rows of 2 segments each, watching orientation. Sew rows together to complete the Rail Fence block.

FROM THE PAGES OF
Lizzy Albright and the Attic Window, Chapter 1

She folded up the well-loved, but not tattered, snuggle quilt that Granny made for her when she started first grade. Granny explained the quilt featured the Rail Fence pattern, but Lizzy never thought it looked much like any fence she had ever seen.

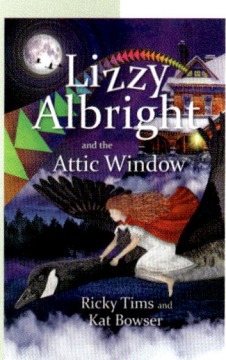

Designed by Ricky Tims

20 Pickle Dish

To anyone who has ever seen a cut-glass pickle dish, the similarity in design to this quilt block is striking. It's an old pattern, with some quilts of this design dating back at least as far as the 1860s. However, the Pickle Dish name is a relatively new one, with first mentions arising in the early 1930s. Lizzie's grandmother may have called it by another name, but she knew a classic and lovely quilt block design when she saw one!

FABRICS NEEDED

Fabric 1 (light triangles): 12″ x 15″
Fabric 2 (points): 10″ x 15″
Fabric 3 ("melon" centers): 6″ x 8″
Fabric 4 ("melon" corners): 6″ x 6″
Fabric 5 (background): 10″ x 16″

CUT

Fabric 1
  48 squares 1⅝″ x 1⅝″ (areas 1, 3, 5, 7, 9, and 11)
Fabric 2
  40 squares 1⅝″ x 1⅝″ (areas 2, 4, 6, 8, and 10)
Fabric 3
  4 Template A
Fabric 4
  8 Template B
Fabric 5
  4 Template C

OPTIONAL NOTE TO HAND PIECERS

The foundation pieced arcs and the A, B, and C patches can be sewn together by hand if you prefer, for beautiful accurate results and a relaxing sewing experience!

SEW

Pickle Dish is a challenging design. Taking your time as you sew will pay off in an accurate, flat, square block.

Make 8 accurate paper copies of the arc foundation. Foundation piece the arcs. Trim edges even with outer lines on the foundation paper. Sew a line of stay stitching inside the outer seam allowances (about ⅛″ from the raw edges). Carefully remove the foundation paper from the backs of the arcs.

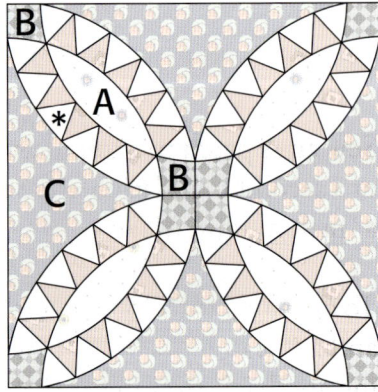

Pickle Dish Assembly

Pickle Dish
Color Options

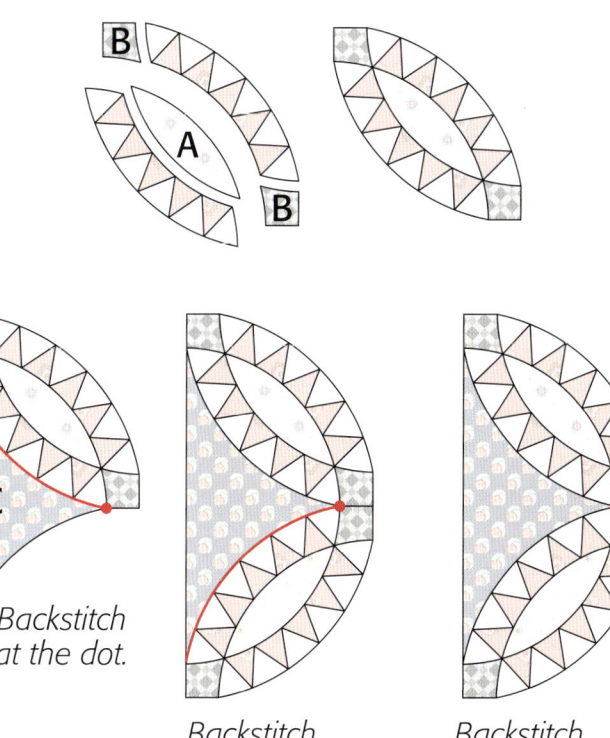

FROM THE PAGES OF
Lizzy Albright and the Attic Window, Chapter 10

Pulling his wand from his coat pocket, Gethric pointed it toward Cedric's motorbie, and said, "Calliope! Alamah!" Gethric's spell forced air through Cedric's ooga horn and it suddenly began playing "The Pickle Dish" reel. The ooga's wheezing honk made the tune sound as if it were being performed by an asthmatic duck playing a kazoot, which made them roar with laughter.

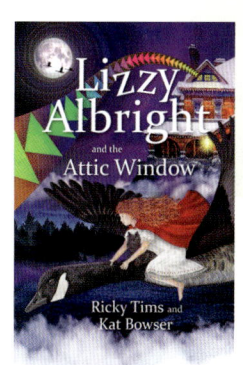

Sew an A patch to a foundation arc. Stitch B patches to ends of a second foundation arc. Sew the 2 units together to make a "melon" unit. Make 4.

To assemble the block, begin by sewing together a melon and a C patch, starting at the outside of the block and ending and backstitching at the dot. Repeat to add a second melon. Sew the seam between the 2 B patches, starting at the dot. Make 2 of these half-block units.

Designed by Ricky Tims

20 cont.

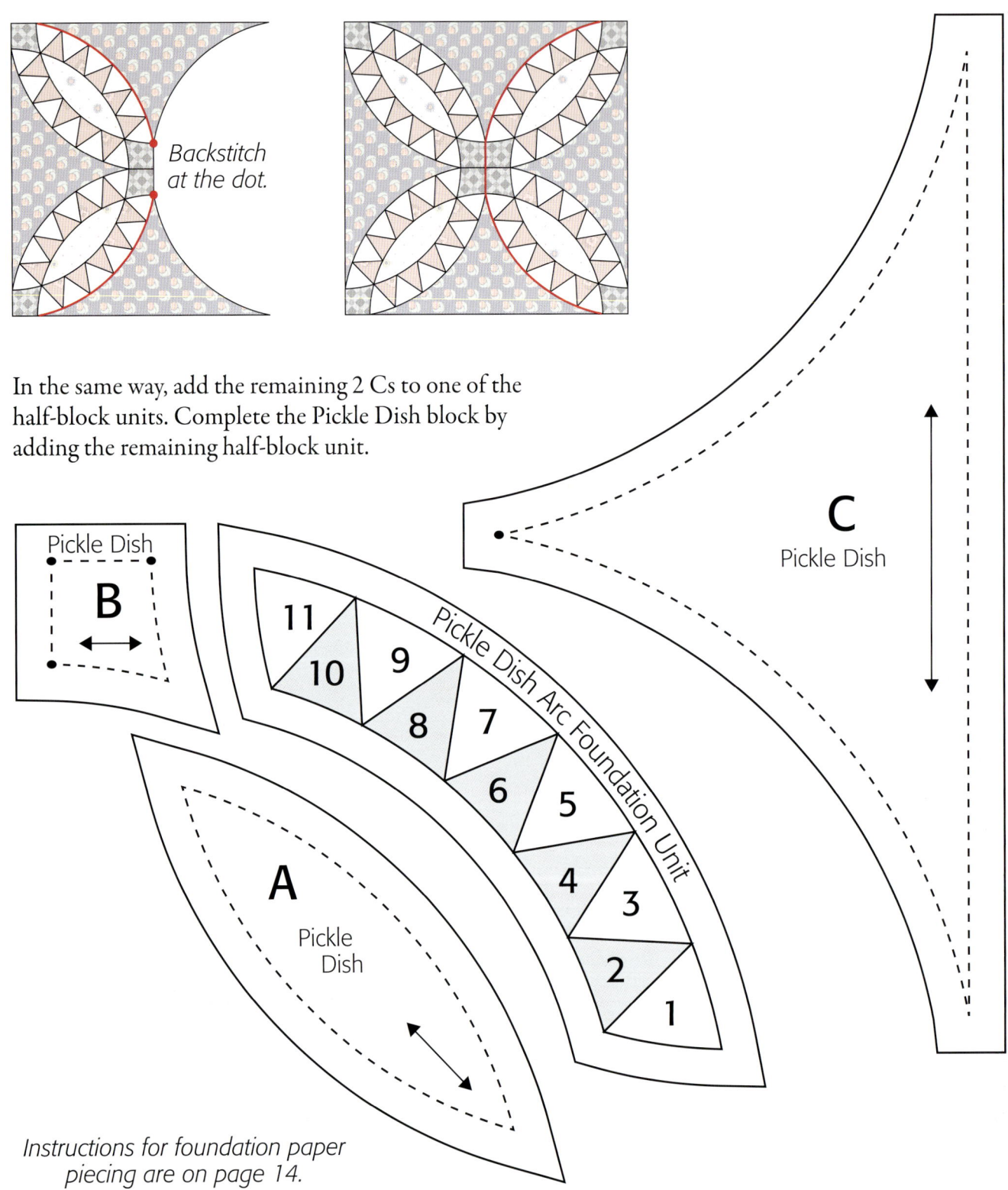

Backstitch at the dot.

In the same way, add the remaining 2 Cs to one of the half-block units. Complete the Pickle Dish block by adding the remaining half-block unit.

Instructions for foundation paper piecing are on page 14.

Granny's 1930 Sampler: From the Lizzy Albright Collection

21 Puss in the Corner

This name has been applied to a number of different quilt block designs, including this one, essentially 4 uneven nine-patches combined. There are stunning antique quilts dating from the early 1900s that use this block pattern.

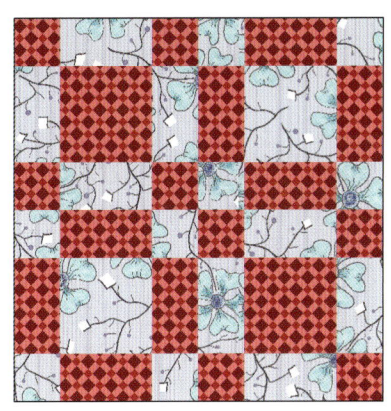

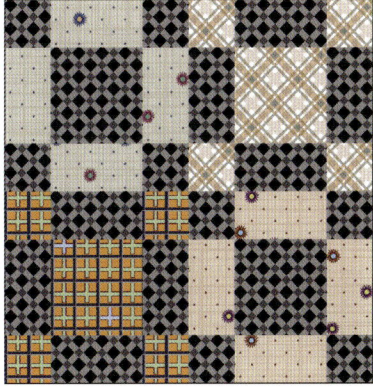

Puss in the Corner Color Options

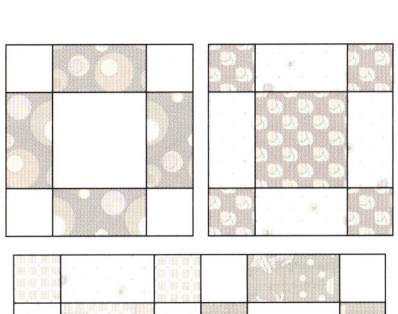

Puss in the Corner Assembly

FABRICS NEEDED

Fabrics 1 and 2 (backgrounds):
 7" x 8" *each*
Fabrics 3, 4, 5, and 6 (prints):
 4" x 7" *each*

CUT

Fabric 1
 8 squares 1½" x 1½" (A)
 2 squares 2½" x 2½" (C)
Fabric 2
 8 rectangles 1½" x 2½" (B)
Fabrics 3 and 4 – *cut from each:*
 4 rectangles 1½" x 2½" (B)
Fabrics 5 and 6 – *cut from each:*
 4 squares 1½" x 1½" (A)
 1 square 2½" x 2½" (C)

SEW

For each quarter-block, arrange 3 rows of 3 patches each, watching fabric placement closely. Sew the rows and press seams to darker fabrics. Sew the rows together to make the quarter-block. Make 4 total.

Sew 2 rows of 2 quarter-blocks each. Sew the rows together to complete the Puss in the Corner block.

Designed by Ricky Tims

22 Sunbonnet Sue

Quilt blocks featuring this iconic image began appearing as early as the 1800s, but their popularity soared following the publication of the Sunbonnet Babies Primers in the early 20th century. Sunbonnet Sue was one of the characters used in these books to teach children how to read. Other common names for the design include Dutch Doll, Bonnie Bonnet, and Sun Bonnet Baby.

FABRICS NEEDED

Fabric 1 (background): 9″ x 9″ (A)
Fabric 2 (shoe, bonnet): 6″ x 6″
Fabric 3 (dress, ribbon): 7″ x 7″
Fabric 4 (hand): 2″ x 2″
Fabric 5 (sleeve): 2″ x 3″

CUT

Fabric 2
    1 *each* Templates B and F
Fabric 3
    1 *each* Templates C and G
Fabric 4
    1 Template D
Fabric 5
    1 Template E

SEW

Prepare appliqué patches for your favorite technique. Finger-press fabric 1 A square in half vertically and horizontally; use folds as placement guide. Appliqué B through G in alphabetical order to make the Sunbonnet Sue block. Press well.

Trim the block to 8½″ square, centering Sue.

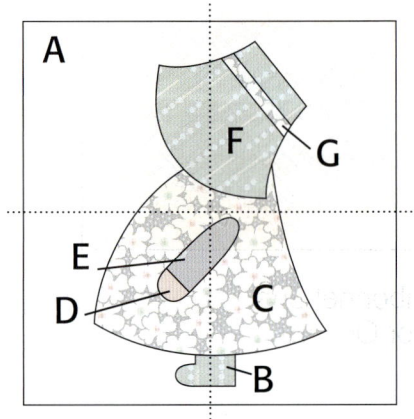

Sunbonnet Sue Assembly

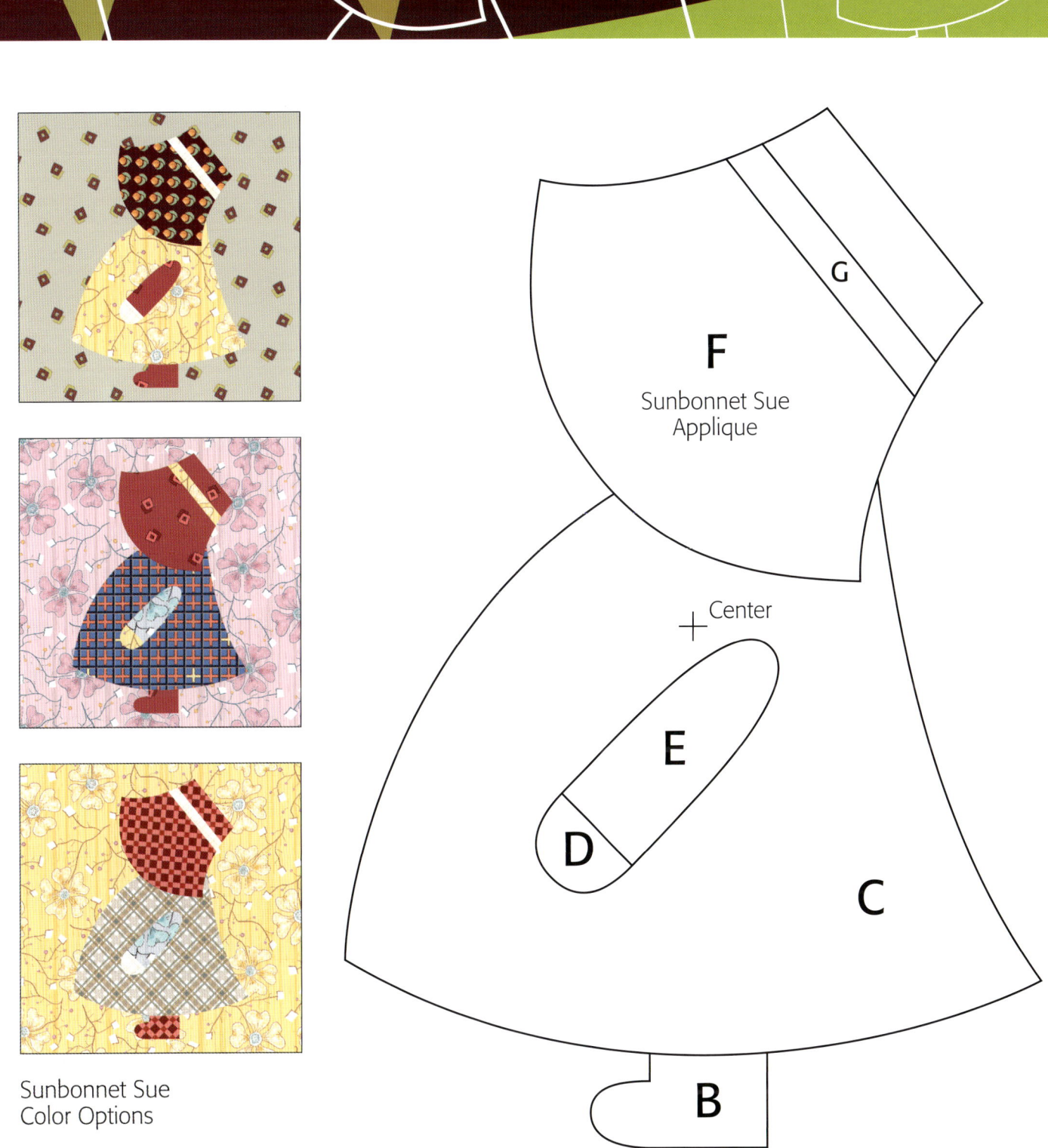

Sunbonnet Sue
Color Options

Appliqué instructions are on page 16. Add 3/16" turn-under allowance to appliqué patches. Reverse applique shapes if using freezer paper or fusible web techniques.

Designed by Ricky Tims   65

23 Friendship Star

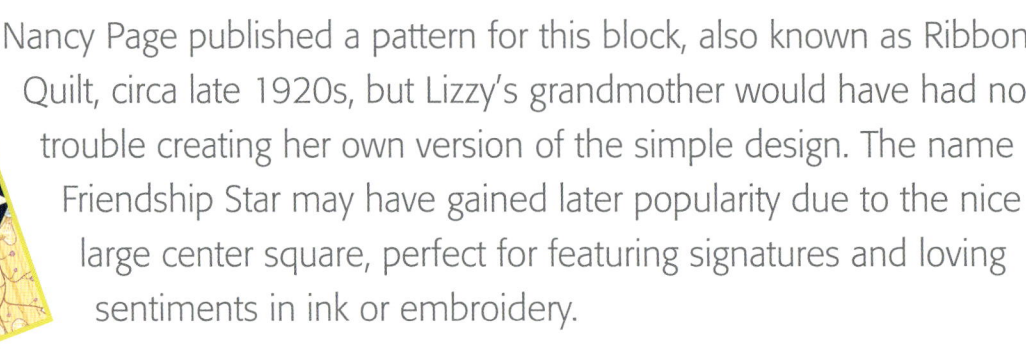

Nancy Page published a pattern for this block, also known as Ribbon Quilt, circa late 1920s, but Lizzy's grandmother would have had no trouble creating her own version of the simple design. The name Friendship Star may have gained later popularity due to the nice large center square, perfect for featuring signatures and loving sentiments in ink or embroidery.

FABRICS NEEDED

Fabric 1 (corners): 5" x 9"
Fabric 2 ("ribbons"): 9" x 9"
Fabric 3 (star): 9" x 9"

CUT

Fabric 1
  2 squares 4" x 4" (A)
Fabric 2
  4 squares 4" x 4" (A)
Fabric 3
  2 squares 4" x 4" (A)
  1 Template B

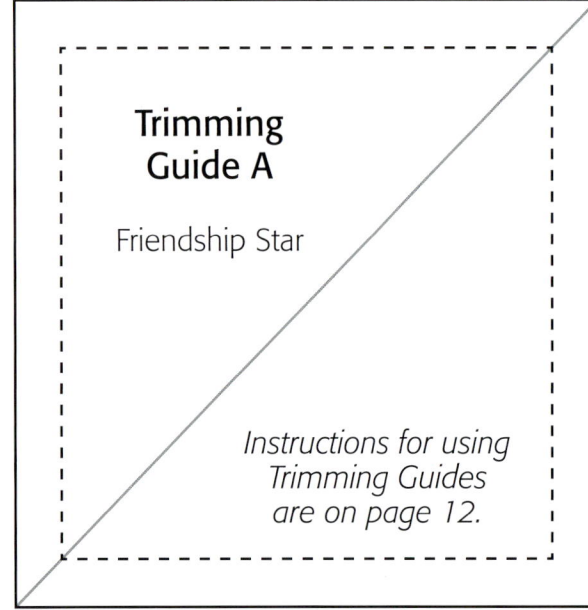

Trimming Guide A
Friendship Star

Instructions for using Trimming Guides are on page 12.

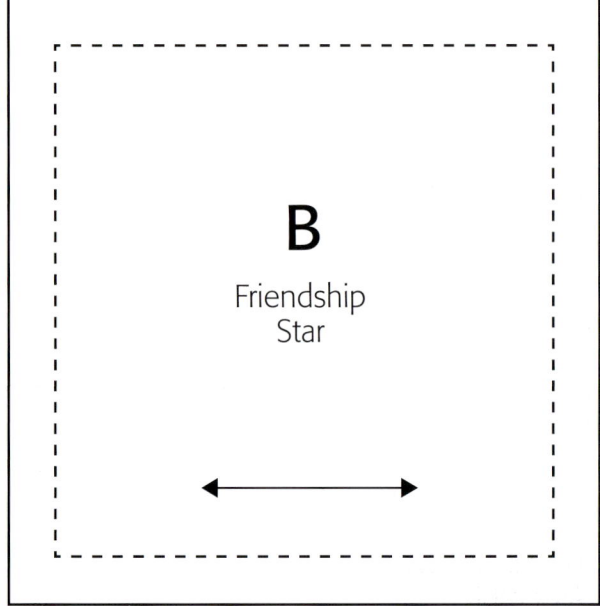

B
Friendship Star

Granny's 1930 Sampler: From the Lizzy Albright Collection

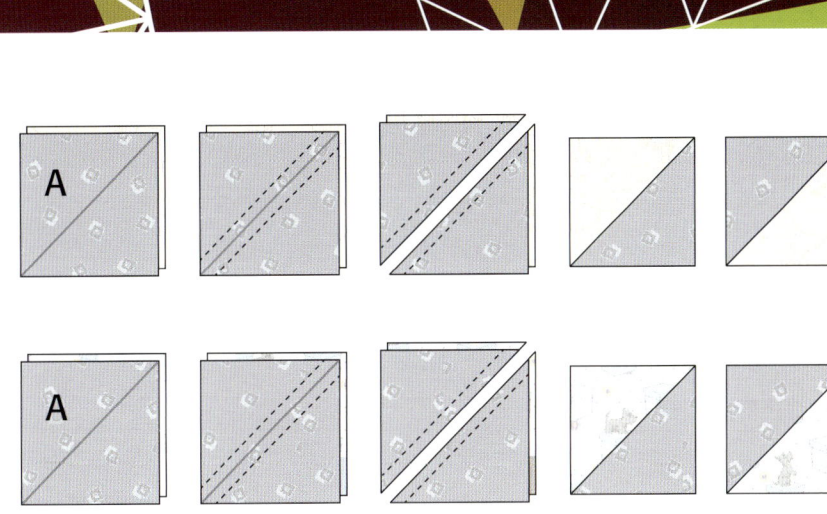

SEW

Draw a diagonal line on the wrong side of each of the 4 fabric 2 squares. Place a marked square on a fabric 1 square, right sides together. Sew ¼" seam on each side of the marked line; cut apart on the marked line. Open the 2 pieced squares and press the seams to the darker fabric. Repeat to make 4 pieced squares of the fabric 1/fabric 2 combination. Also make and press 4 pieced squares of the fabric 3/fabric 2 combination.

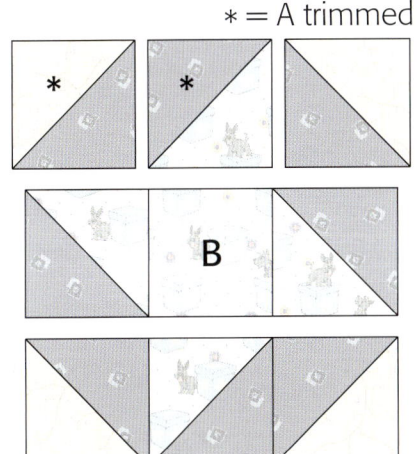

Friendship Star Assembly

Using the Trimming Guide, trim all the pieced squares to size, aligning seam lines with the gray line on the Guide.

Sew 3 rows using the pieced squares and fabric 3 B. Sew the rows together to complete the Friendship Star block.

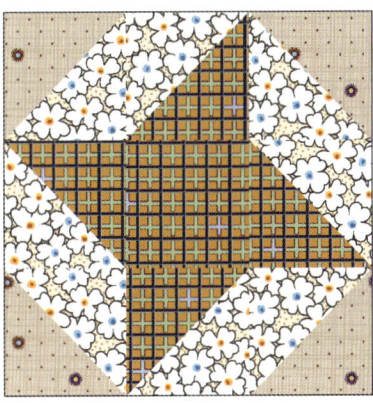

Friendship Star Color Options

Designed by Ricky Tims   67

24 Kaleidoscope

This quilt block design is also known as Octagons, Will of the Wisp, and The Windmill, and it dates back to at least the beginning of the 20th century. The version in this quilt requires 3 fabrics with good value contrast to highlight the dynamics of the design.

FABRICS NEEDED

Fabric 1 (dark triangles): 11″ x 11″
Fabric 2 (light triangles): 11″ x 11″
Fabric 3 (corners): 5″ x 9″

CUT

Fabric 1
    4 squares 4¾″ x 4¾″ (area 1)
Fabric 2
    4 squares 4¾″ x 4¾″ (area 2)
Fabric 3
    2 squares 4″ x 4″ ◳ (area 3)

SEW

Make 4 accurate paper copies of the foundation. Foundation piece the units. Trim edges even with outer lines on the foundation paper.

Sew 2 units together to make a half-block. Make 2. Sew half-blocks together to complete the Kaleidoscope block.

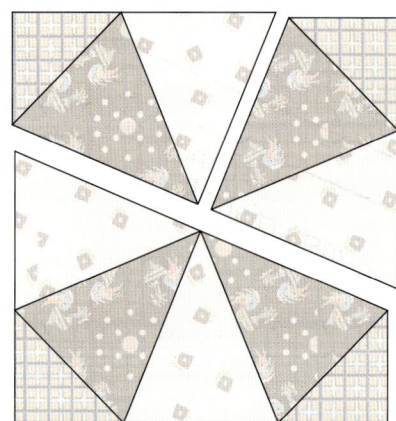

Kaleidoscope Assembly

68   Granny's 1930 Sampler: From the Lizzy Albright Collection

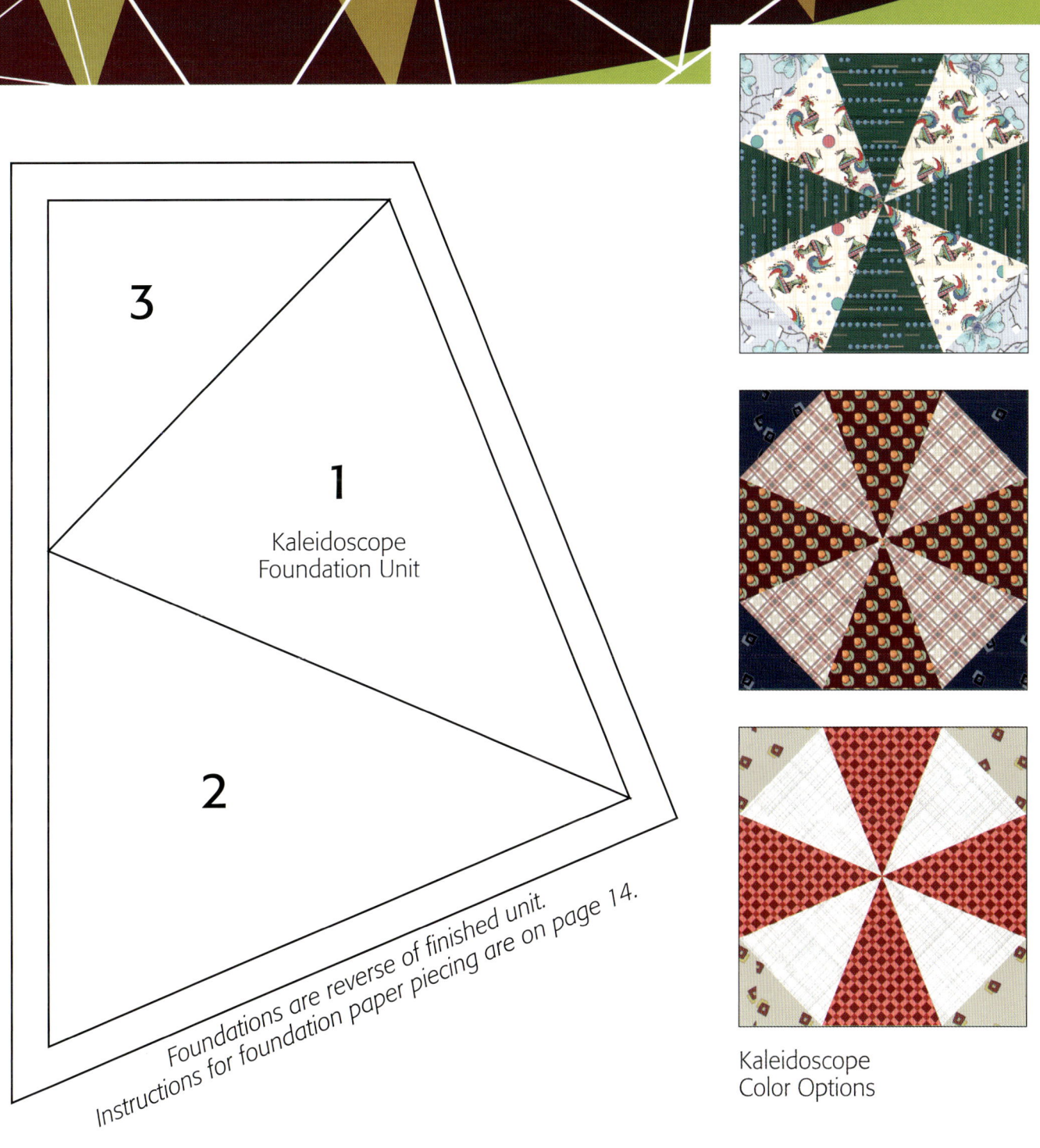

1 Kaleidoscope Foundation Unit

Foundations are reverse of finished unit. Instructions for foundation paper piecing are on page 14.

Kaleidoscope Color Options

Sew a line of stay stitching inside the outer seam allowance (about 1/8″ from the raw edges). Carefully remove the foundation paper from the back of the block.

Designed by Ricky Tims

25 Hunter's Star

Also known as Indian Arrowhead, this block is another gem popular in the 1920s and 30s. Select two fabrics with good contrast to show off all your perfectly foundation-pieced points!

FABRICS NEEDED

Fabrics 1 (light) and 2 (dark): 13″ x 14″ or fat eighth (9″ x 20-22″ cut of fabric) *each*

CUT

Fabrics 1 and 2 – *cut from each*:
  2 squares 4 1/2″ x 4 1/2″ ◻ (area 4)
  4 rectangles 1 3/4″ x 4″ (area 1)
  8 rectangles 1 3/4″ x 3″ (areas 2 and 3)

SEW

Make 4 accurate copies of each foundation. Foundation piece the units. Trim edges even with outer lines on the foundation papers.

Sew together 2 units, 1 of each fabric arrangement, to make a quarter-block. Make 4.

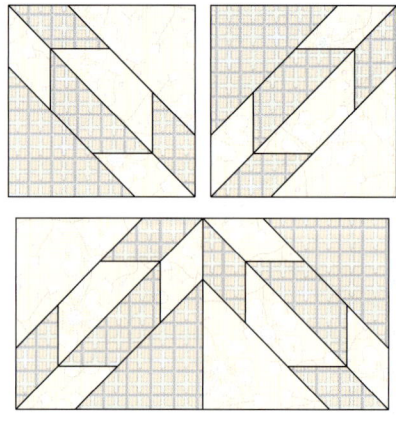

Hunter's Star Assembly

Granny's 1930 Sampler: From the Lizzy Albright Collection

Stitch 2 rows of 2 quarter-blocks each, and then sew rows together to complete the Hunter's Star block.

Sew a line of stay stitching inside the outer seam allowance (about 1/8″ from the raw edges). Carefully remove the foundation paper from the back of the block.

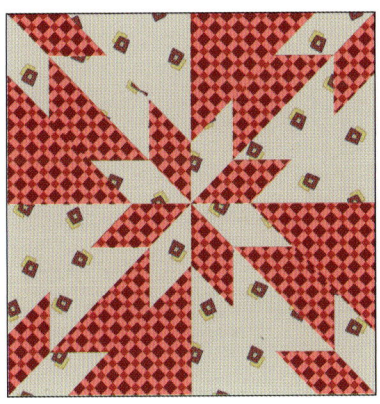

Hunter's Star Color Options

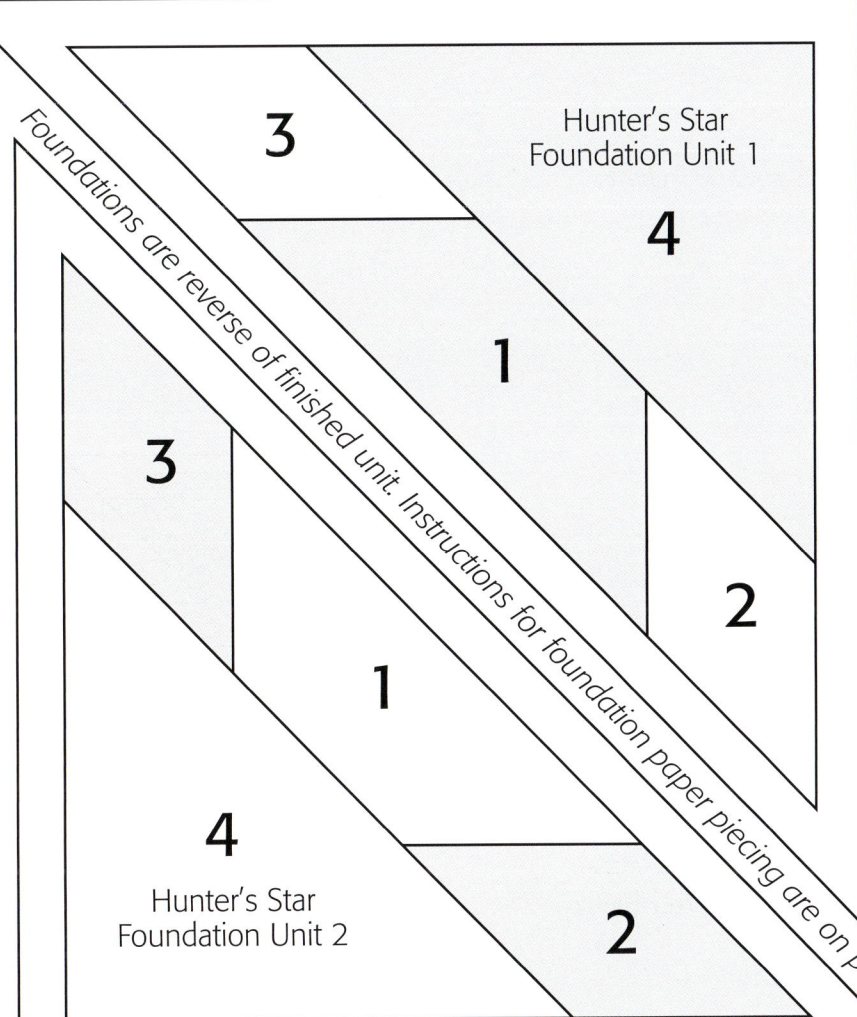

Designed by Ricky Tims

26 Bear Paw

Here's another quilt block of seemingly endless names! In this case Bear's Foot, Hand of Friendship, Cat's Paw, The Best Friend, and Tea Leaf Design have all been used to refer to what is most commonly called Bear Paw. Many patterns for this block were published in the 1920s and 30s.

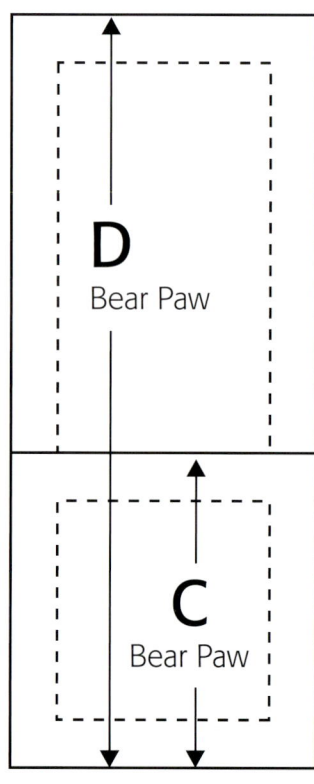

FABRICS NEEDED

Fabric 1 (light large triangles): 5" x 8"
Fabric Group 2 (dark large triangles, points, center square): assorted prints totaling 10" x 14"
Fabric 3 (background): 10" x 15"

CUT

Fabric 1
　*2 squares 3½" x 3½" (A)
Fabric Group 2 – *cut a total of:*
　*2 squares 3½" x 3½" (A)
　8 squares 2¼" x 2¼" (B)
　1 Template C
Fabric 3
　8 squares 2¼" x 2¼" (B)
　4 Template C
　4 Template D

*These instructions will yield 2 sets of 2 matching large pieced squares. For a scrappier look like in the sample quilt, you may wish to make more large pieced squares. If so, cut more fabric 1 and 2 A squares.

SEW

Draw a diagonal line on the wrong side of each of the fabric 1 squares. Place a marked square on a fabric 2 A square, right sides together. Sew ¼" seam on each side of the marked line; cut apart on the marked line. Open the 2 large pieced squares and press the seams to the darker fabric. Repeat to make 4 large pieced squares of the fabric 1/fabric 2 combinations. Using Trimming Guide A, trim all the large pieced squares to size, aligning seam lines with the gray line on the Guide.

Instructions for using Trimming Guides are on page 12.

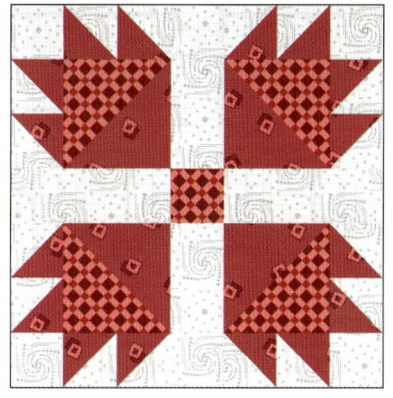

Bear Paw
Color Options

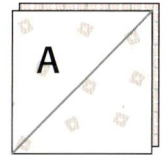 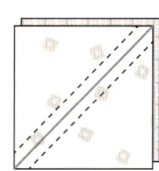 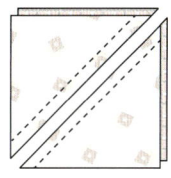 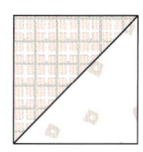 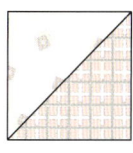

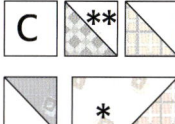

* = A trimmed
** = B trimmed

Using the same technique and the fabric 2 and fabric 3 B squares, make 16 small pieced squares. Trim to size using Trimming Guide B.

To make a "paw" unit, arrange and sew 2 rows using 1 fabric 3 C, 4 assorted small pieced squares, and 1 large pieced square. Sew the rows together. Make 4 units.

Arrange and sew 3 rows using the 4 units, 4 fabric 3 Ds, and the fabric 2 C. Sew the rows together to complete the Bear Paw block.

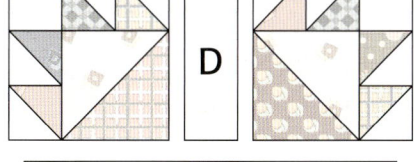

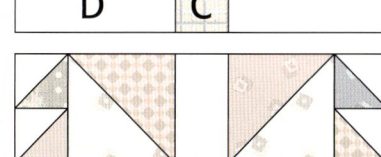

Bear Paw
Assembly

FROM THE PAGES OF
Lizzy Albright and the Attic Window, Chapter 30

Lizzy was frozen and her mouth was agape. Her eyes scanned her rescuer. She had seen bears at the Kansas City Zoo, but she had no idea they were this big up close. The bear reached out to brush Lizzy's hair from her face. Lizzy winced with uncertainty, but the bear's paw was so gentle, her fears melted and she relaxed.

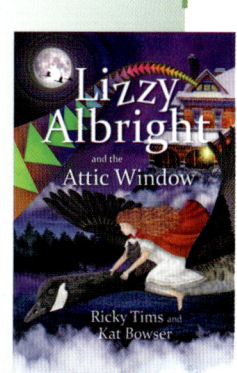

Designed by Ricky Tims

27 Spools

Quilt blocks depicting thread spools date back as least as far as the 1900s. Whether called Spools or Spool, Empty Spool, or Diversion, this intriguing pattern is a tribute to the sewing arts and a sweet domestic touch in Lizzy's grandmother's quilt.

FABRICS NEEDED

Fabric 1 (dark spools): 7″ x 10″
Fabric 2 (light background): 7″ x 10″
Fabric Group 3 (spool centers):
    assorted prints totaling 7″ x 7″

CUT

Fabrics 1 and 2 – *cut from each:*
    8 Template B
Fabric Group 3 – *cut a total of:*
    4 squares 2½″ x 2½″ (A)

SEW

Using a rotary ruler and fabric marking pencil, mark match points at all 4 corners of the wrong sides of the 4 As, ¼″ from raw edges. Also transfer match points from Template B to wrong sides of 16 fabric Bs.

Sew fabric 2 Bs to top and bottom of an A, starting and stopping seams at match points. Sew fabric 1 Bs to sides

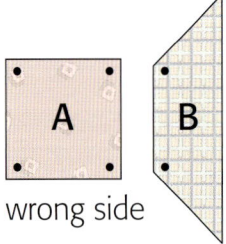
wrong side
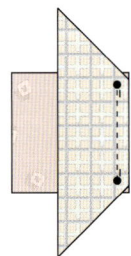
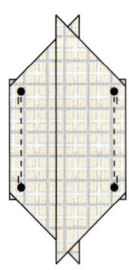

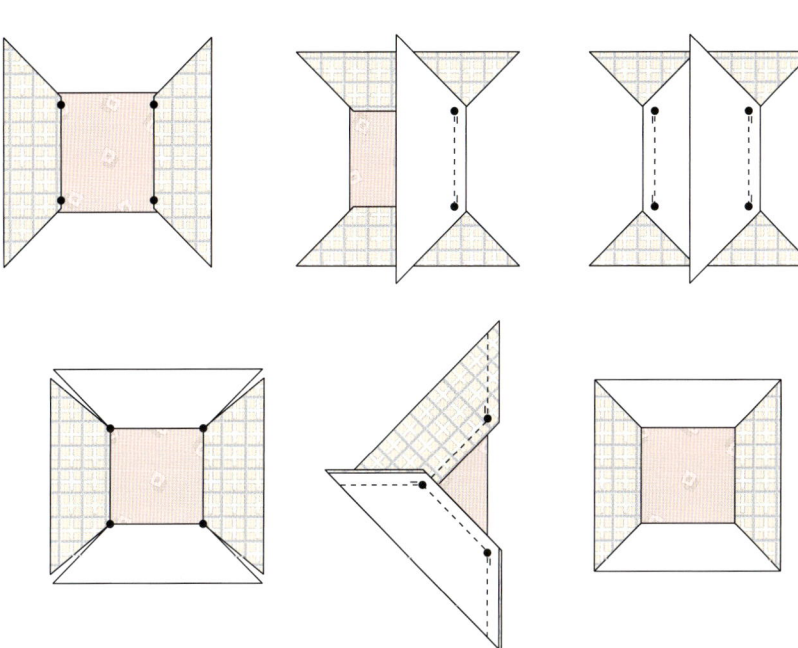

in the same way. Stitch from match points to the outer edge of a mitered corner seam. Repeat for 4 total mitered seams to make a spool unit. Repeat sewing steps to make 4 total spool units.

Sew 2 rows of 2 spools each, watching orientation. Sew the rows together to complete the Spools block.

Spools
Color Options

Spools Assembly

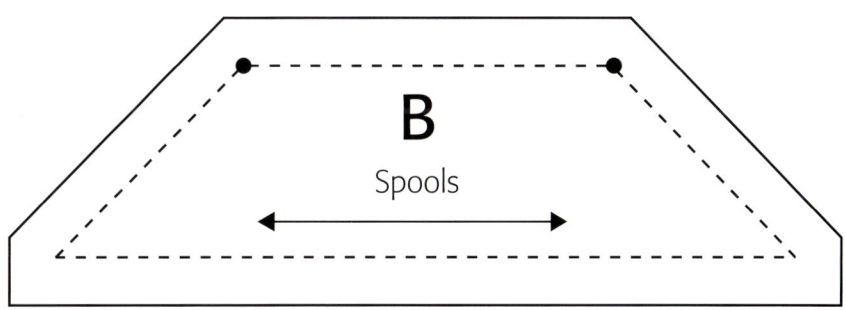

Designed by Ricky Tims

28 Pineapple

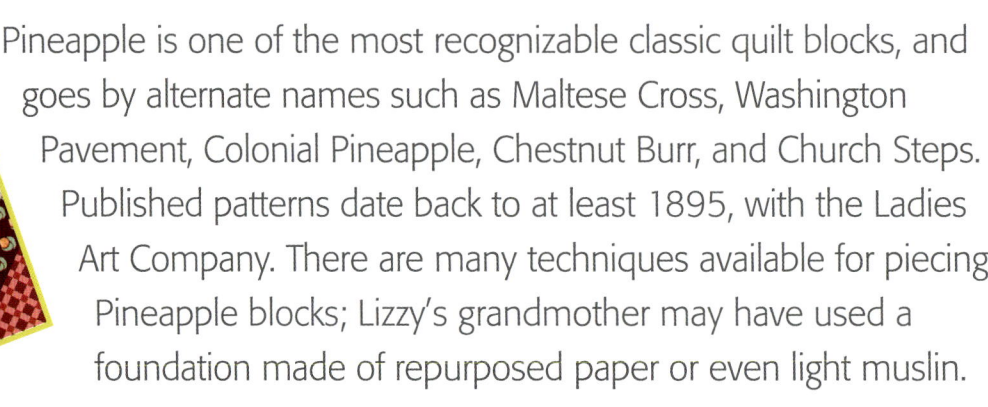

Pineapple is one of the most recognizable classic quilt blocks, and goes by alternate names such as Maltese Cross, Washington Pavement, Colonial Pineapple, Chestnut Burr, and Church Steps. Published patterns date back to at least 1895, with the Ladies Art Company. There are many techniques available for piecing Pineapple blocks; Lizzy's grandmother may have used a foundation made of repurposed paper or even light muslin.

FABRICS NEEDED

Fabric Group 1 (center square and dark "pineapples"): assorted prints totaling ¼ yard

Fabric 2 (light "pineapples"): ⅛ yard

CUT

Fabric Group 1 – *cut a total of:*
  2 squares 3½" x 3½" ◲ (area 10)
  1 square 2½" x 2½" (area 1)
  4 strips 1½" x 5" (area 9)
  4 strips 1½" x 4⅜" (area 7)
  4 strips 1½" x 3¾" (area 5)
  4 strips 1½" x 3" (area 3)

Fabric 2
  4 strips 1½" x 4⅜" (area 8)
  4 strips 1½" x 3¾" (area 6)
  4 strips 1½" x 3" (area 4)
  4 strips 1½" x 2⅜" (area 2)

SEW

Make an accurate paper copy of the foundation (tape copies of half-

Pineapple Color Options

Granny's 1930 Sampler: From the Lizzy Albright Collection

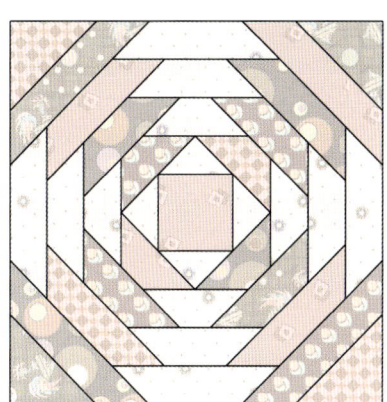

Pineapple Assembly

foundations together as shown). Use a glue stick to adhere the *wrong* side of the center square to the *unprinted* side of the foundation on area 1. Foundation piece the remainder of the block in numerical order. Trim edges even with outer lines on foundation paper.

Sew a line of stay stitching inside the outer seam allowance of the block (about 1/8″ from the raw edges). Carefully remove all foundation paper from the back of the block.

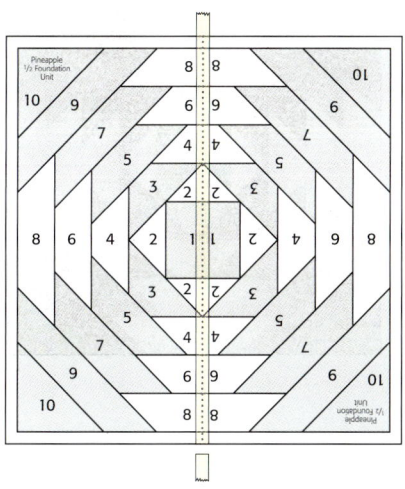

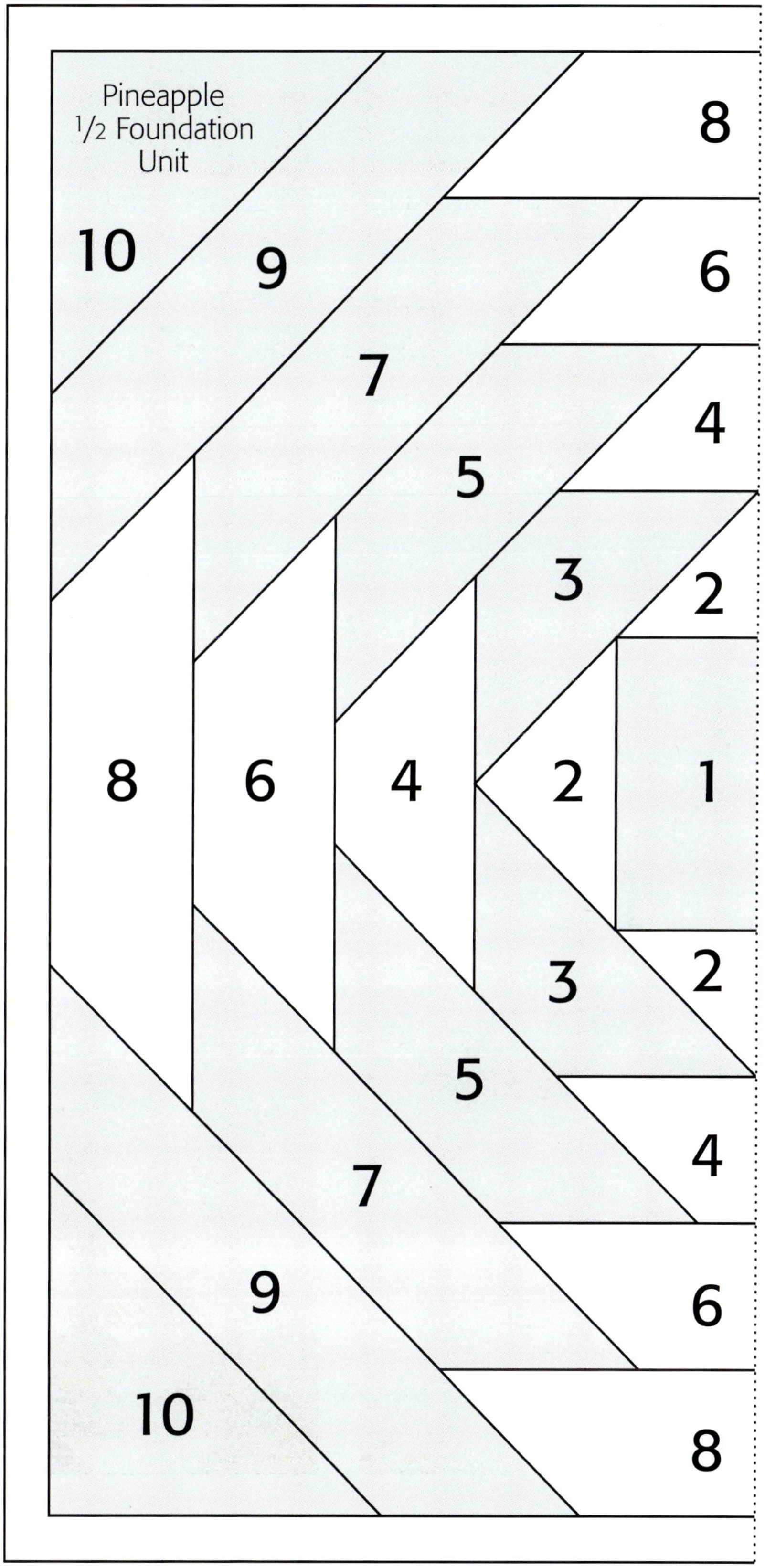

Designed by Ricky Tims   77

29 Fifty-Four Forty or Fight

The unusual name of this quilt block is a reference to President Polk's 1844 campaign slogan having to do with the fight over the latitude of the proposed Oregon border. Grandma's Star and Railroad Quilt are other names for this design.

FABRICS NEEDED

Fabrics 1 and 2 (four-patches):
   5″ x 12″ each
Fabric 3 (star point background):
   8″ x 8″
Fabric 4 (star points): 8″ x 10″

CUT

Fabrics 1 and 2 – *cut from each:*
   10 squares 2″ x 2″ (A)
Fabric 3
   4 squares 3½″ x 3½″ (area 1)
Fabric 4
   8 rectangles 2¼″ x 3½″
   (areas 2 and 3)

Fifty-Four Forty or Fight
Color Options

Instructions for using Trimming Guides are on page 12.
Instructions for foundation paper piecing are on page 14.

Granny's 1930 Sampler: From the Lizzy Albright Collection

SEW

Sew together 2 each fabric 1 and fabric 2 As to make a four-patch. Make 5. Trim all four-patches to size using the Trimming Guide.

Make 4 accurate paper copies of the foundation. Use a glue stick to adhere the *wrong* side of the fabric 3 square to the *unprinted* side of the foundation on area 1. Foundation piece the remainder of the unit. Trim edges even with outer lines on foundation paper. Foundation piece 4 units. Sew a line of stay stitching inside the outer seam allowance of each unit (about 1/8″ from the raw edges). Carefully remove all foundation paper from the back of the units.

Sew 3 rows using the 5 four-patches and the 4 foundation units. Sew the rows together to complete the Fifty-Four Forty or Fight block.

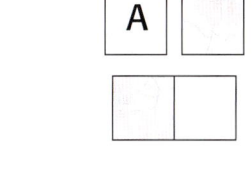

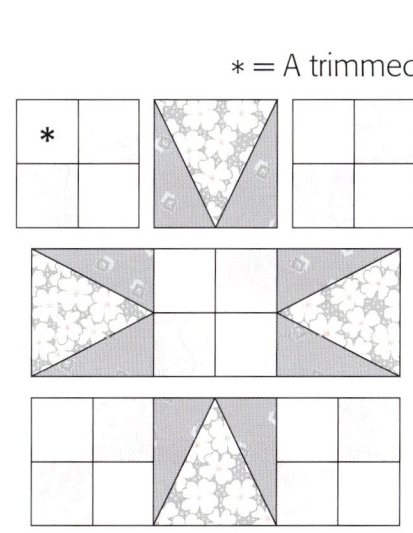

Fifty-Four Forty or Fight Assembly

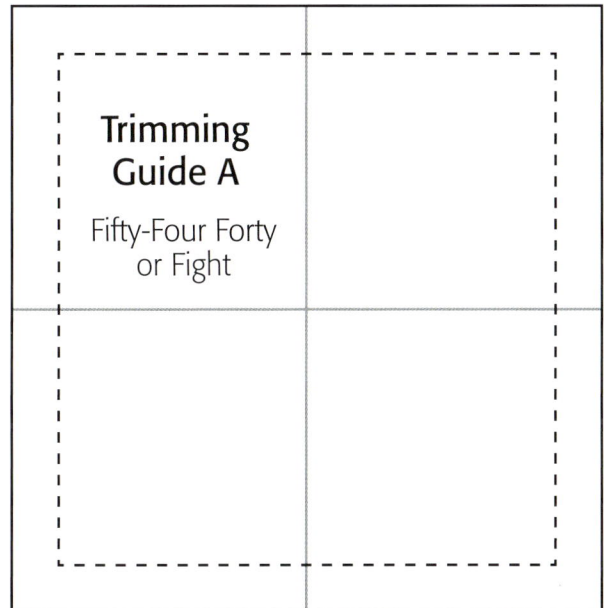

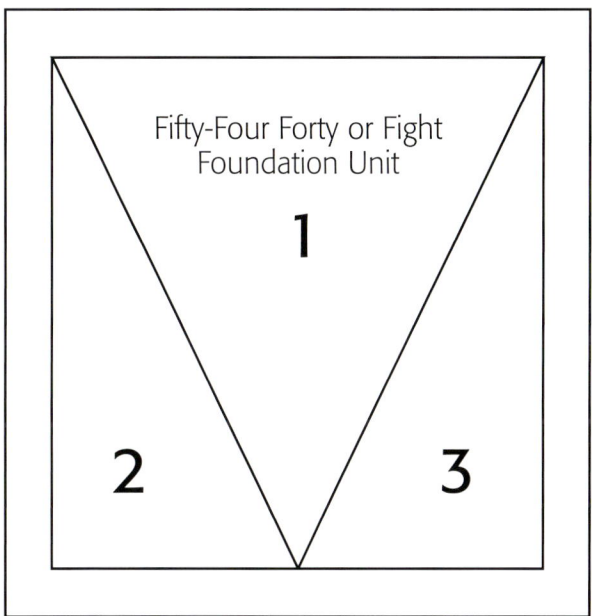

Designed by Ricky Tims

30 Honey Bee

Another Depression-era favorite, this quilt block design is also known as Blue Blazes. Patterns date back to the 1840s with a plain square as the center; the variation with a nine-patch center developed in the 1920s. It's a great block for anyone wanting to try a bit of appliqué!

FABRICS NEEDED

Fabric 1 ("bees" and center square): 6″ x 10″
Fabric 2 (background): 8″ x 18″ or fat eighth (9″ x 20-22″ cut of fabric)
Fabric 3 ("wings"): 6″ x 9″

CUT

Fabric 1
 5 squares 1 3/4″ x 1 3/4″ (A)
 4 Template E
Fabric 2
 4 rectangles 2 5/8″ x 4 1/4″ (B)
 4 squares 2 5/8″ x 2 5/8″ (C)
 4 squares 1 3/4″ x 1 3/4″ (A)
Fabric 3
 8 Template D

SEW

Use fabric 1 and fabric 2 As to sew 3 rows of 3 squares each. Sew rows together to make a nine-patch.

Arrange 3 rows using 4 C squares, 4 B rectangles, and nine-patch. Sew rows, and then sew the 3 rows together. Press seams open.

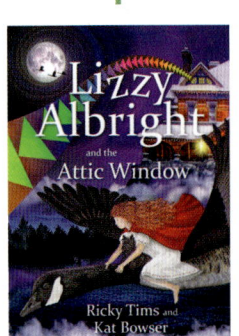

FROM THE PAGES OF
Lizzy Albright and the Attic Window, Chapter 40

She found the Honey Bee block. "Queen Beatrice? Oh no!" she exclaimed with disdain, and quickly moved on to the others.

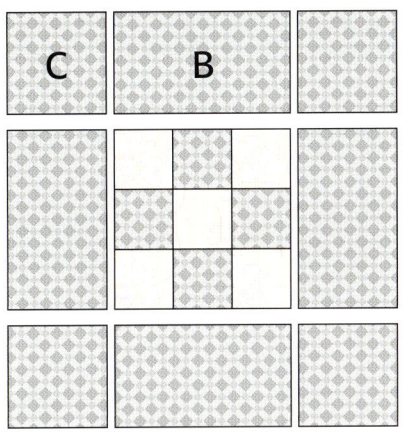
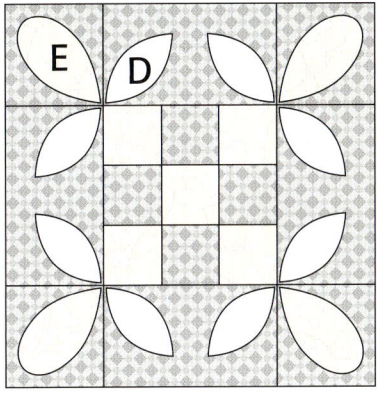

Honey Bee
Assembly

Appliqué D and E shapes to corners to complete the Honey Bee block.

APPLIQUÉ TIP

Position the D and E appliqué shapes just a few threads away from the corner seams to make stitching easier and help keep the block flat.

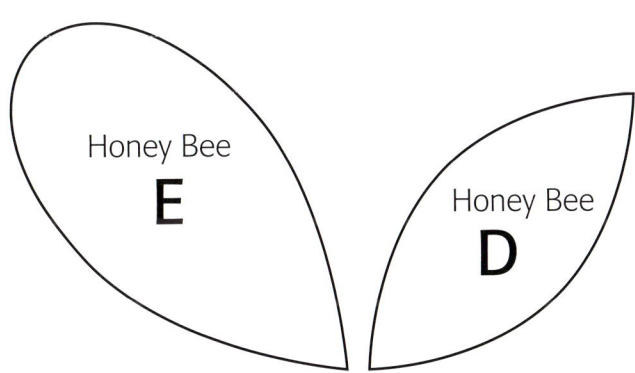

Honey Bee
Color Options

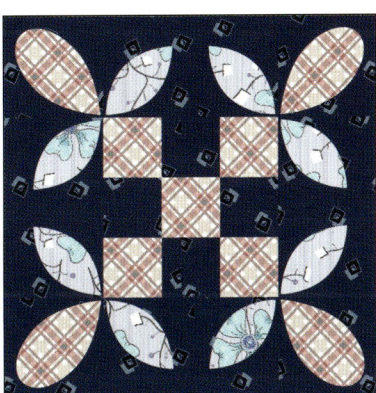

Designed by Ricky Tims   81

31 Moon Over the Mountain

Although we couldn't find any historical references to this block predating 1949, it's likely it was being made much earlier. The theme of moon over the mountain ties in well with Lizzy's grandmother's quilt and story.

FABRICS NEEDED

Fabric 1 (background): 8½" x 8½" (A)
Fabric 2 (moon): 8" x 8"
Fabric 3 (mountain): 6" x 9"

CUT

Fabric 2
　*1 Template B
Fabric 3
　**1 Template C

*Add 3/16" turn under allowance if using a turned-edge appliqué technique.
**Add 3/16" turn under allowance to slanted sides if using a turned-edge appliqué technique.

SEW

Finger-press the A square in half both horizontally and vertically. Using the creases as placement guides, pin or glue-baste the B moon on the A square, centering. Appliqué in place.

Pin or glue-baste the C mountain to the block, aligning bottom edges. Appliqué the slanted sides in place.

Sew a line of stay stitching inside the bottom seam allowance of the block (about 1/8" from the raw edge).

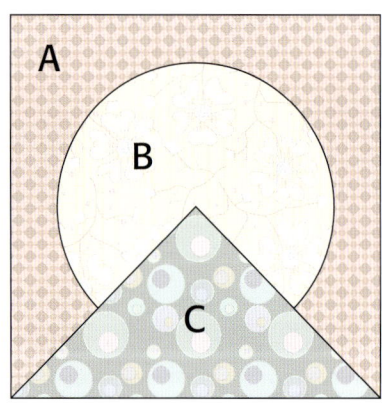

Moon Over the Mountain Assembly

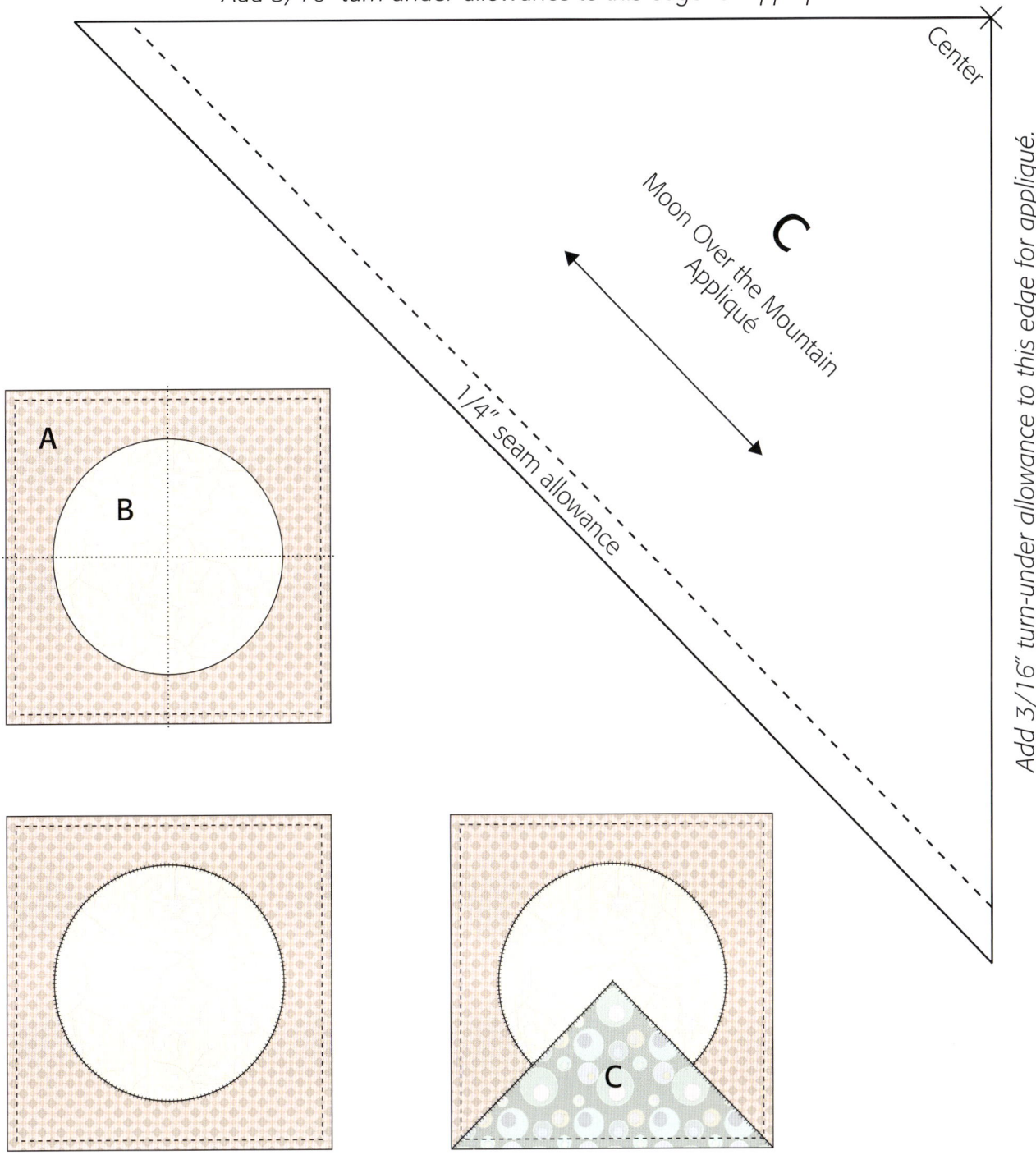

Designed by Ricky Tims

31 cont.

B

Moon Over the Mountain
Appliqué

+
Center

Add 3/16″ turn-under allowance to appliqué patches.

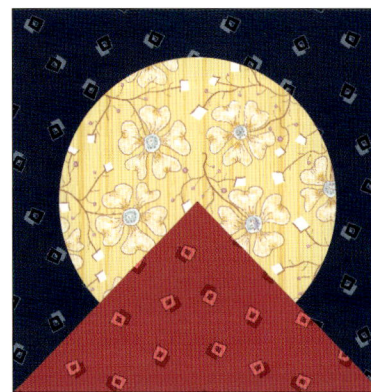

Moon Over the Mountain
Color Options

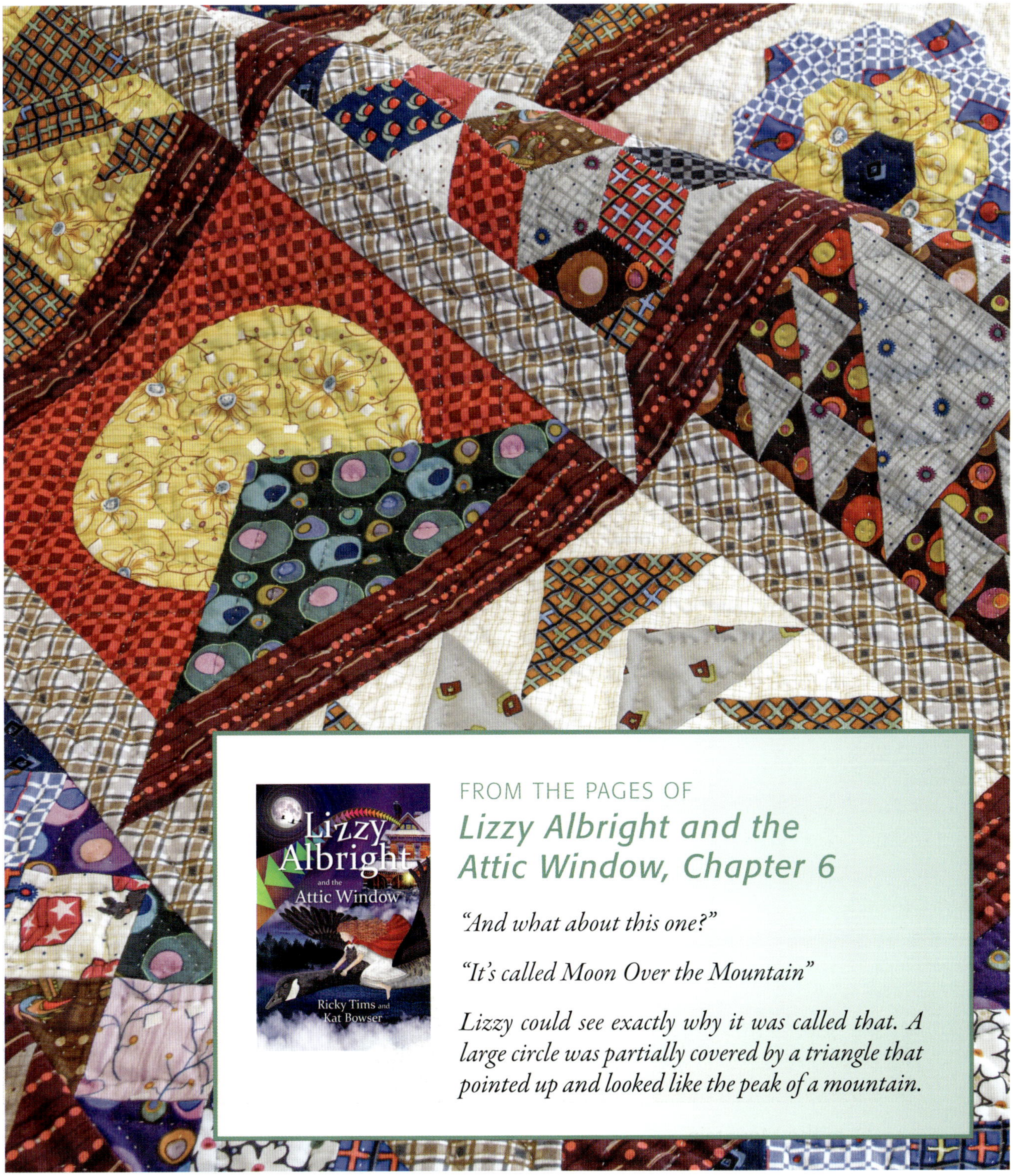

FROM THE PAGES OF
Lizzy Albright and the Attic Window, Chapter 6

"And what about this one?"

"It's called Moon Over the Mountain"

Lizzy could see exactly why it was called that. A large circle was partially covered by a triangle that pointed up and looked like the peak of a mountain.

Designed by Ricky Tims

32 Tumbling Blocks

This optical-illusion design dates back at least to the 1850s, when *Godey's Lady's Book* published a pattern for it. Other names include Baby's Blocks, Building Blocks, Cubework, and Disappearing Blocks.

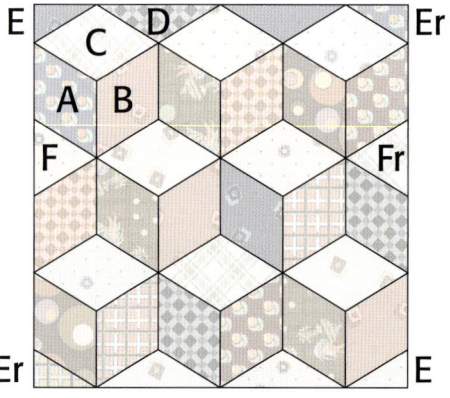

Tumbling Blocks Assembly

FABRICS NEEDED

Fabric Group 1 (lights): assorted prints totaling 10″ x 12″
Fabric Group 2 (darks): assorted prints totaling 11″ x 11″
Fabric Group 3 (mediums): assorted prints totaling 7″ x 10″

*CUT

Fabric Group 1 – *cut a total of:*
   8 Template C
   2 Template D
   1 *each* Templates E, Er, F, and Fr
Fabric Group 2 – *cut a total of:*
   9 Template A
   2 Template D
   1 *each* Templates E and Er
Fabric Group 3 – *cut a total of:*
   9 Template B

*See English paper piecing instructions on page 17 before cutting fabric.

SEW

Referring to the instructions on page 17, make templates of shapes A, B, C, D, E/Er, and F/Fr. Prepare fabric patches for English paper piecing.

Sew together a light C, dark A, and medium B to make a tumbling block. Make 8 total.

Sew together a light F and a medium B to make a left-side partial block. Sew together a light Fr and a dark A to make a right-side partial block.

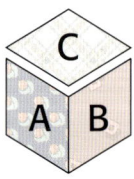
Make 8

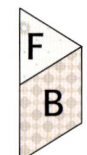
Make 1

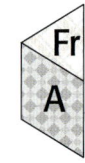
Make 1

Tumbling Blocks Color Options

Sew blocks and partial blocks together in 3 rows. Stitch the rows together. Sew D triangles to the top and bottom edges. Add E and Er patches to the corners to complete the Tumbling Blocks block. Stay stitch approximately 1/8″ from block raw edges. Remove templates from the back of the block if you have not already done so.

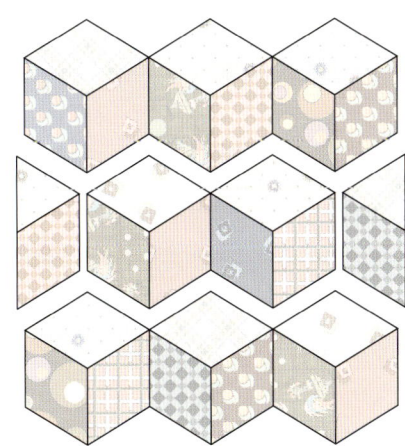

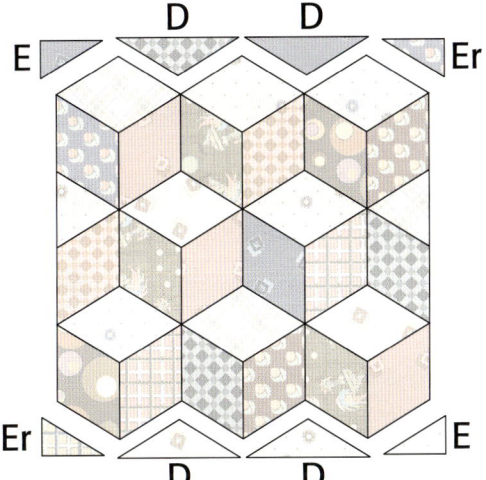

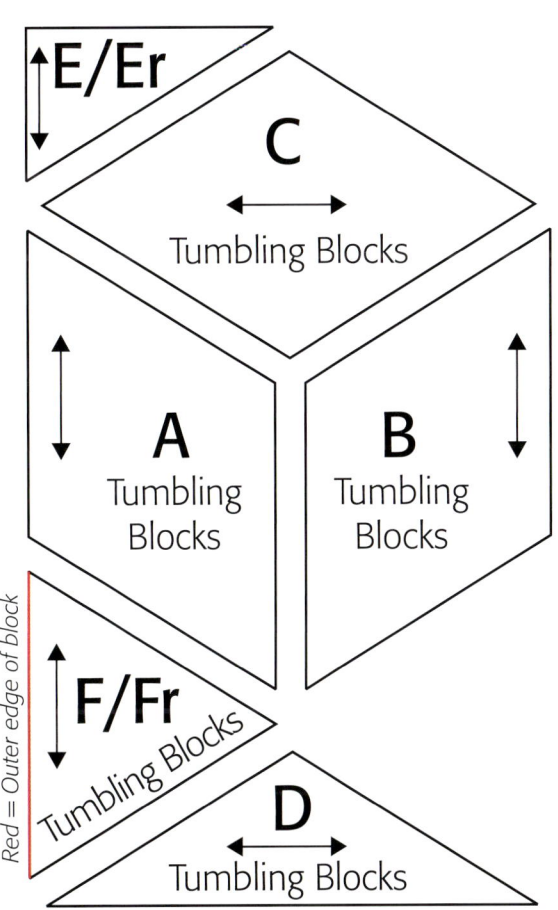

Red = Outer edge of block

Designed by Ricky Tims

33 Grandmother's Flower Garden

Vintage examples of quilts made in this much-loved design include an 1813 beauty in the collection of the Shelburne Museum, and an 1866 quilt made in Kentucky and documented by Mary Washington Clarke. The variety of hexagon quilt patterns is nearly infinite, and common names also include Honeycomb and Mosaic.

FABRICS NEEDED

Fabric 1 (background): 9" x 9" (A)
Fabric 2 (center hexagon): 2" x 2"
Fabric 3 (middle hexagons): 5" x 7"
Fabric 4 (outer hexagons): 7" x 9"

*CUT

Fabric 2
    1 Template B
Fabric 3
    6 Template B
Fabric 4
    12 Template B

*See English paper piecing instructions on page 17 before cutting fabric.

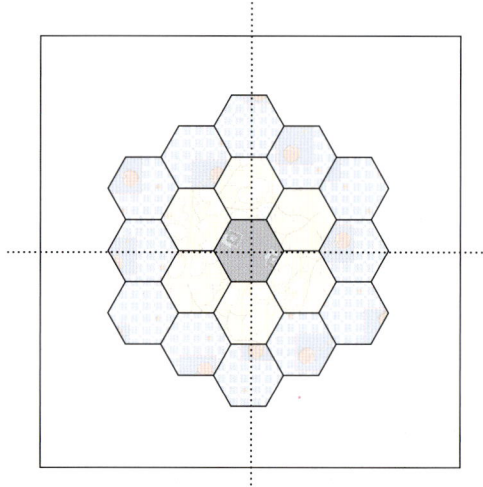

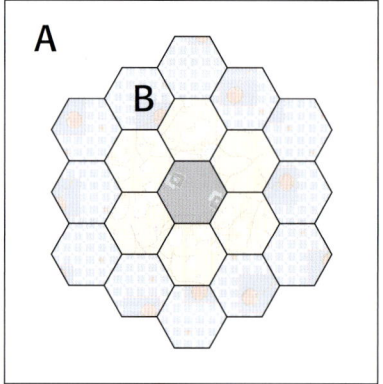

Grandmother's Flower Garden Assembly

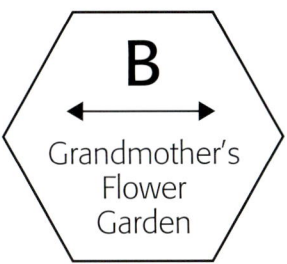

Add 3/16˝ turn-under allowance to edges.

SEW

Referring to the instructions on page 17, make B templates. Prepare fabric patches for English paper piecing.

Sew 6 fabric 3 B shapes to the fabric 2 B shape, and then join the adjacent sides of the fabric 3 shapes to make the flower center. In the same way, add 12 fabric 4 B shapes to complete the flower. Using the templates as a pressing guide, press the outer turn-under allowance to the wrong side of the flower. Use spray starch or sizing to stabilize the fabric. You can trim the edges of the fabric slightly to reduce bulk during pressing if needed.

Finger-press the fabric 1 square in half both horizontally and vertically. Using the creases as a placement guide, pin or glue-baste the flower to the background. Appliqué in place.

Trim the block to 8½˝ square, centering the flower, to complete the Grandmother's Flower Garden block.

Grandmother's Flower Garden Color Options

Designed by Ricky Tims

34 Grandmother's Fan

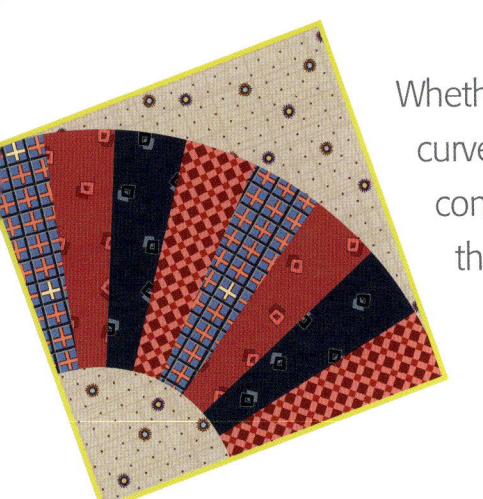

Whether the outer edge of the fan is scalloped, pointed, or a smooth curve as in this block, it's easy to see how the design got its most common name! Published patterns date back to at least 1911 for this lovely block.

OPTIONAL NOTE TO PIECERS

The foundation pieced fan and the A and B patches can be sewn together in the traditional way if you prefer, instead of appliquéing the curved edges together. Be sure to align the match points with the arc seams, and use an accurate 1/4″ seam allowance so your block is square!

FABRICS NEEDED

Fabric Group 1 (fan): assorted prints totaling 12″ x 13″
Fabric 2 (background): 9″ x 14″

CUT

Fabric Group 1 – *cut a total of:*
    8 rectangles 2 1/2″ x 5 3/4″
       (for foundation piecing)
Fabric 2
    1 *each* Templates A and B

SEW

Make 2 accurate paper copies of the 1/2 arc foundation. Foundation piece the 1/2 arcs. Trim edges even with outer lines on the foundation paper. Sew the 1/2 arcs together to complete the fan. Sew a line of stay stitching inside the outer seam allowance (about 1/8″ from the raw edges). Carefully remove the foundation paper from the back of the fan.

To make pressing guides, trace A and B shapes *without seam allowances on the curved edges* onto heat-resistant template

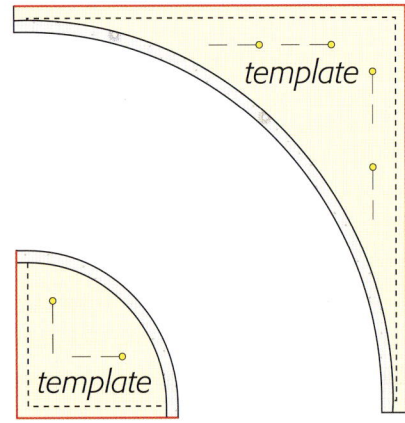

Wrong sides up, align corners.

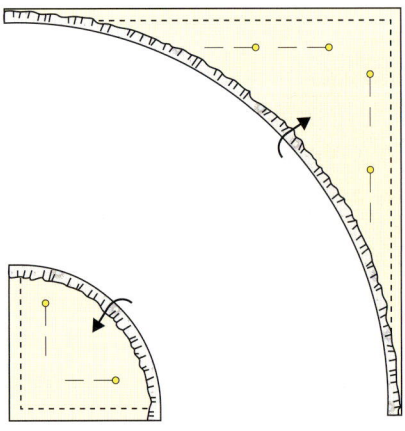

Spray and press.

Granny's 1930 Sampler: From the Lizzy Albright Collection

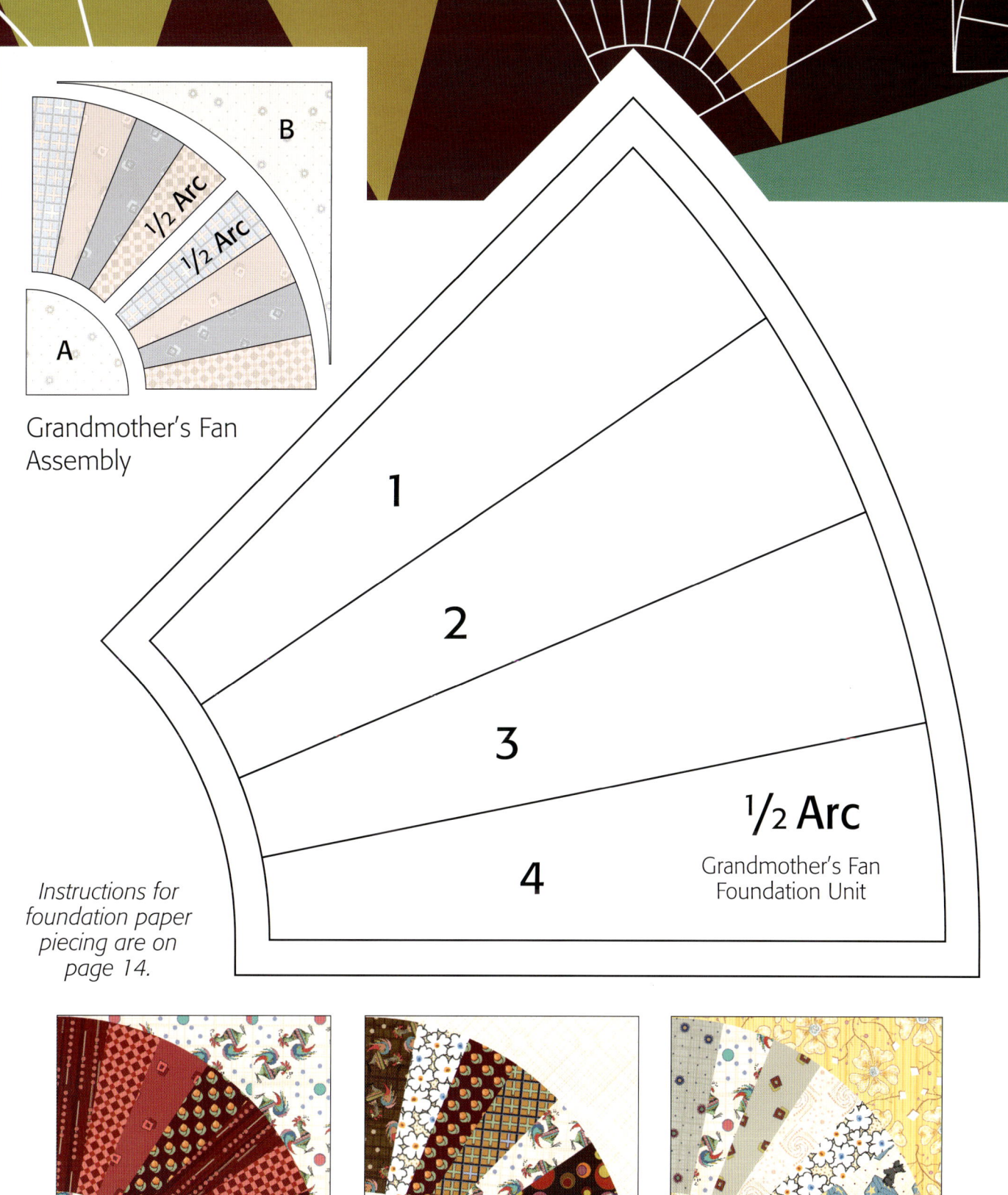

Grandmother's Fan Assembly

Instructions for foundation paper piecing are on page 14.

½ Arc Grandmother's Fan Foundation Unit

Grandmother's Fan Color Options

Designed by Ricky Tims

34 cont.

plastic, light card stock, or a stack of 3 sheets of freezer paper pressed together. Cut out the A and B guides on the traced lines.

Place the B pressing guide on the wrong side of the B patch, aligning the straight raw edges, and use spray starch and an iron to press under the curved edge 1/4″. You will need to clip the curved edge of the fabric to make a smooth curve. Pin or glue-baste the prepared B shape to the larger curve of the fan. Appliqué the curved edge in place.

In the same way, prepare, pin or glue-baste, and appliqué the curve of A to the smaller curve of the fan to complete the Grandmother's Fan block.

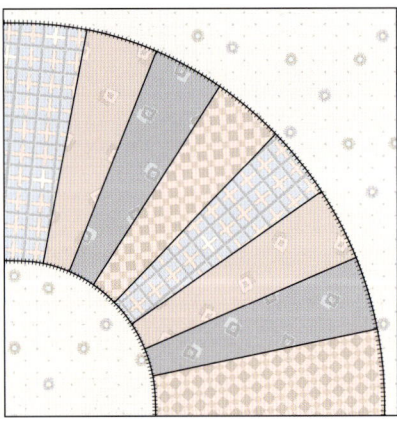

Appliqué curves.

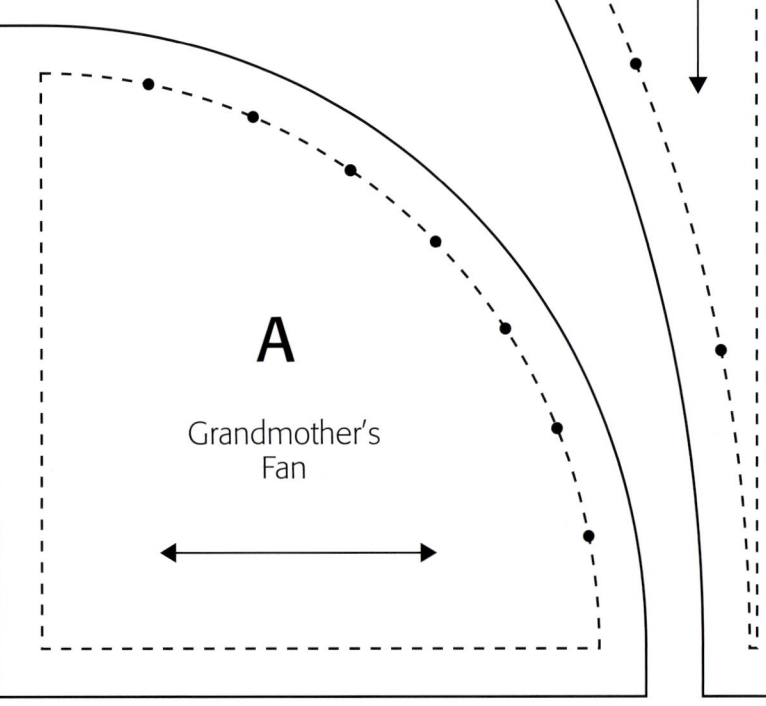

92   Granny's 1930 Sampler: From the Lizzy Albright Collection

FROM THE PAGES OF
Lizzy Albright and the Attic Window, Chapter 6

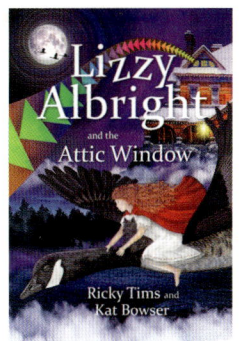

"Where did you get the quilt?" Lizzy asked.

"I made it. I made it many years ago."

Granny went on to explain that she had started making quilt blocks because she was worried. It helped take her mind off her troubles.

"Why were you worried?" asked Lizzy.

"It was a bad time for everyone, not just for me. The country's money system failed and caused the Great Depression—it started in 1929."

She explained that the hardships resulting from that financial disaster lasted a very long time, and many wealthy businessmen lost everything they had. Businesses that for years had been successful crumbled and failed.

Granny emphasized that the McHale family had not escaped the crisis. They too had suffered tremendous financial loss, but luckily, her father had managed to survive the ordeal without losing everything. It took him years to recover, and even so, the McHale family fortune never amounted to what it was before the Great Depression.

Granny also told Lizzy about how prices skyrocketed and that people couldn't afford the most basic necessities. The government gave out rations for eggs, sugar, butter, meat, fish, and cheese. Rationing helped to make sure that those who most needed these things got what they needed—but it almost never seemed to be enough.

"So you see, Lizzy, in many ways, this quilt tells that story."

"What do you mean?" asked Lizzy

"During that time, one of the things people needed most was quilts to keep them warm. They couldn't afford to just go out and buy blankets, and they couldn't even afford to purchase fabric to make a quilt. They had to use what they had on hand. In those days, sacks for seeds, flour, and sugar were made out of cloth. Times got so bad that when the sacks were empty, they were washed, and mothers would use the cloth to make clothes for their children. Some companies started printing pretty designs on the sacks, so at least the kids' clothes looked a bit more cheerful. The leftover scraps were used to make quilts."

"That sounds horrible," sighed Lizzy. "It's so sad."

"It was a sad time for sure, and it was during this worrisome period that I spent most of my time making these quilt blocks. I used pieces of fabric that I found at home. This one was from a dress I once wore." She pointed to a colorful fabric with nesting circles.

Designed by Ricky Tims

35 Delectable Mountains

The name of this design relates to *The Pilgrims Progress*, a Biblical allegory published in 1688. Variations of this quilt block have been around at least since the 1850s. A notable early example survived a harrowing event on the Oregon Trail known as the Lost Wagon Train of 1853. So much history, and such a wonderful quilt block!

FABRICS NEEDED

Fabric 1 (background): 7″ x 14″
Fabrics 2 and 3 ("mountains"):
  7″ x 7″ *each*

CUT

Fabric 1
  2 squares 6 3/8″ x 6 3/8″ (A)
Fabrics 2 and 3 – *cut from each:*
  1 square 6 3/8″ x 6 3/8″

SEW

Draw a diagonal line on the wrong side of each fabric 1 square. Place a fabric 1 and the fabric 2 squares right sides

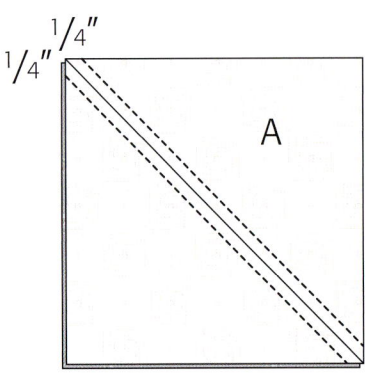

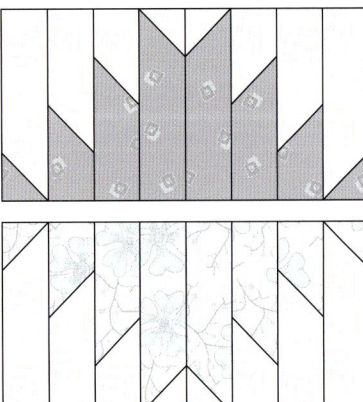

Delectible Mountains Assembly

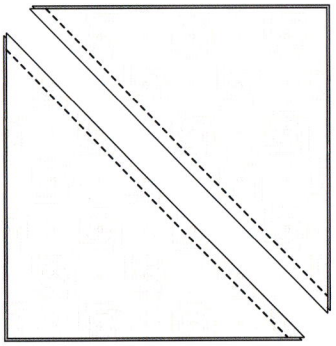

Granny's 1930 Sampler: From the Lizzy Albright Collection

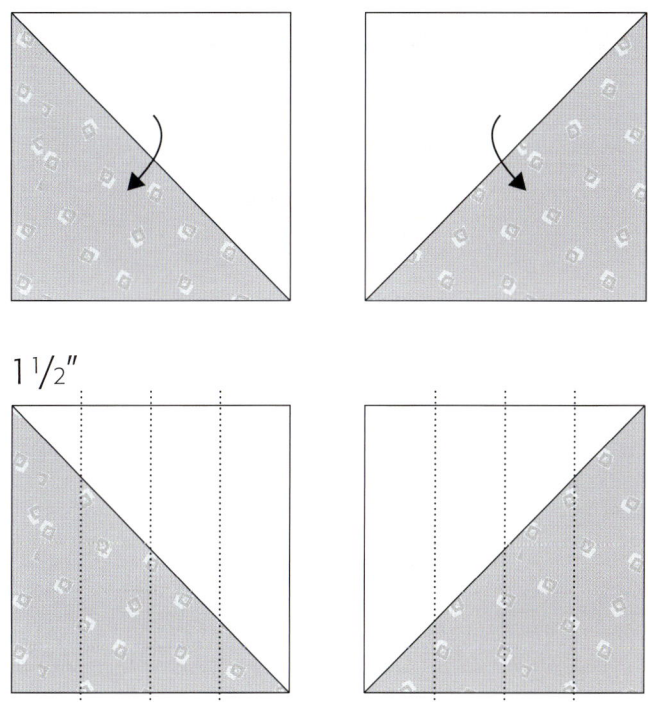

together with marked fabric on top. Sew ¼" from each side of the marked line. Cut apart on the marked line to make 2 pieced squares. Press seams towards the darker fabric.

Place pieced squares on a rotary cutting mat and, referring to the diagram, cut each into 4 strips 1½" wide. Trim each strip as shown to 4½" long.

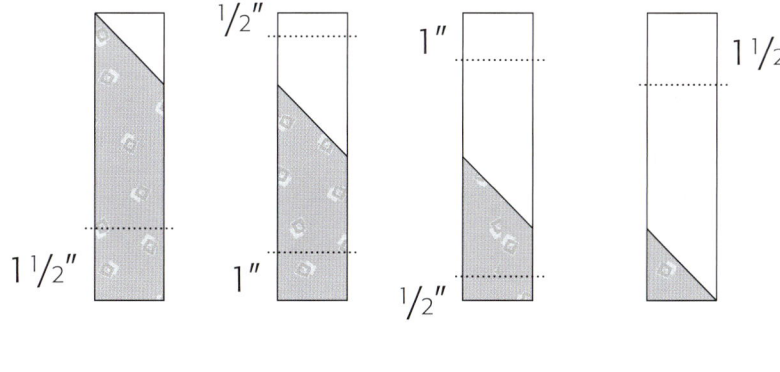

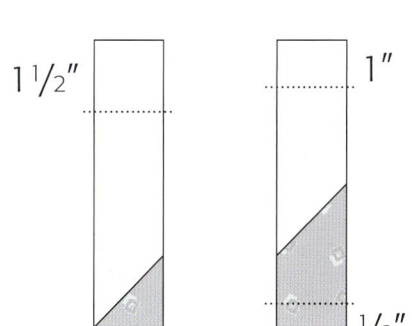
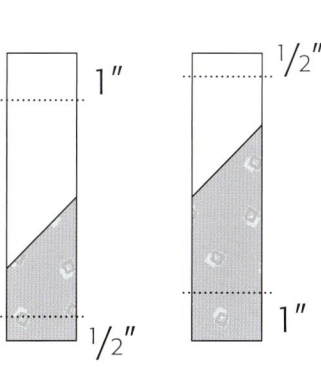
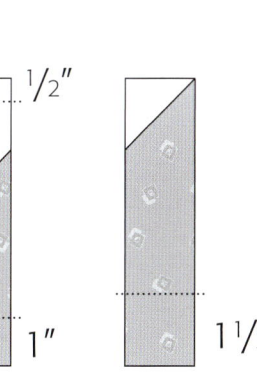

VALUE TIP

When selecting fabrics, pick prints that differ noticeably in value (light vs. medium vs. dark), so the "mountains" are easy to see.

Designed by Ricky Tims

35 cont.

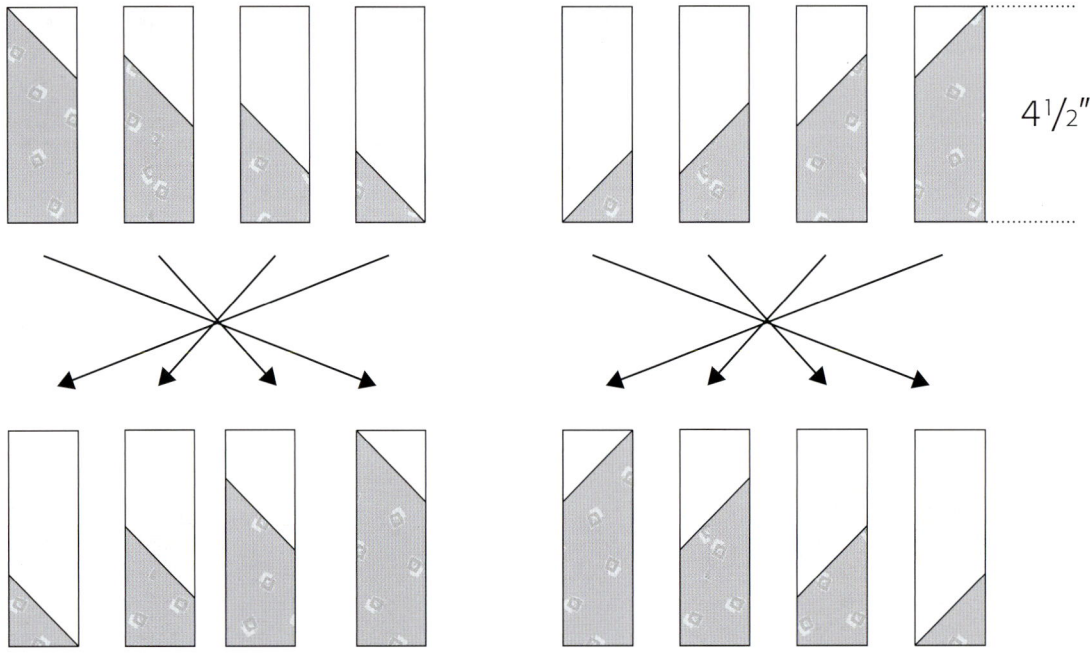

Rearrange strips and then sew them together to make a quarter-block. Make 2. Repeat the process to also make 2 quarter-blocks with fabric 3.

Sew 2 rows of 2 quarter-blocks each. Sew the rows together to complete the Delectable Mountains block.

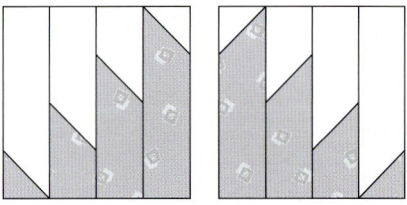

Delectible Mountains
Color Options

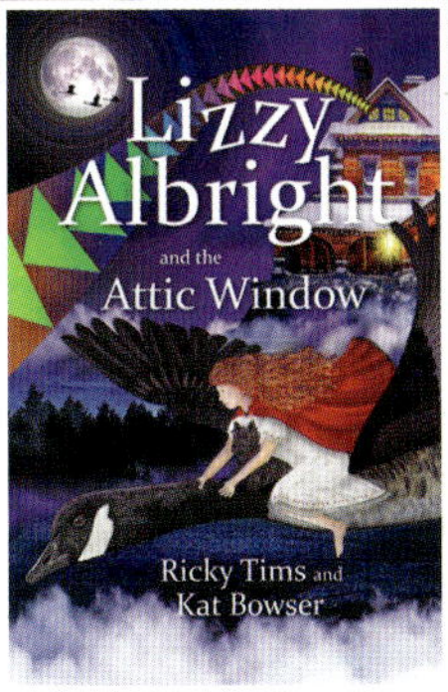

FROM THE PAGES OF
Lizzy Albright and the Attic Window, Chapter 14

Lizzy slammed her eyes shut and crossed her arms tight across her chest. She imagined her bedroom at Granny's house. She envisioned the wallpaper in the room. She could see a gentle snow falling outside the bedroom window. She remembered that she was sleeping under Granny's old quilt. She listed the names of some of the quilt blocks that she remembered and quietly said them out loud—"Bear Paw, Jacob's Ladder, Pickle Dish, and Snail's Trail." She recalled two fabrics in particular. One featured a singing rooster and the other had frolicking Scottish terriers. She was back. She was no longer dreaming. It was time to wake up and open her eyes.

Designed by Ricky Tims

36 Courthouse Steps

In this popular variation on the Log Cabin block, fabric strips are added on opposite sides of the center square for each "round". The Courthouse Steps design has been around at least as far back as the Civil War era. The International Quilt Museum in Lincoln, Nebraska has a number of outstanding quilts of this design in its collection, some dating back to the 1870s.

FABRICS NEEDED

Fabric Group 1 (darks): assorted prints totaling 10″ x 10″

Fabric Group 2 (lights): assorted prints totaling 8″ x 11″

CUT

Fabric Group 1 – *cut a total of:*
 1 square 2½″ x 2½″ (A)
 2 strips 1½″ x 8½″ (E)
 2 strips 1½″ x 6½″ (D)
 2 strips 1½″ x 4½″ (C)

Fabric Group 2 – *cut a total of:*
 2 strips 1½″ x 6½″ (D)
 2 strips 1½″ x 4½″ (C)
 2 strips 1½″ x 2½″ (B)

ACCURACY TIP

For the most accurate, square block, press well after each "round" has been added. After round 1, the unit should measure 4½″ square from raw edge to raw edge. After round 2, it should measure 6½″ square. After round 3, the block should measure 8½″ square.

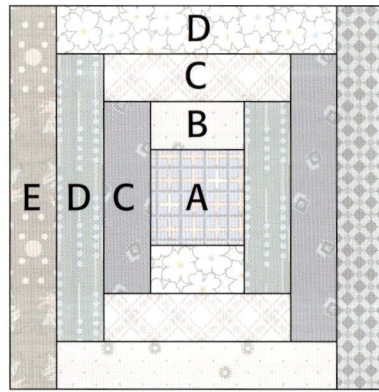

Courthouse Steps Assembly

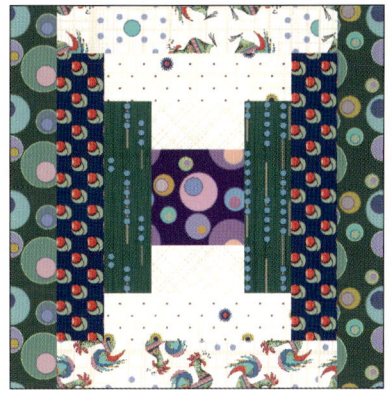

Courthouse Steps
Color Options

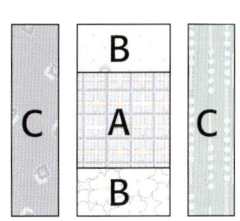
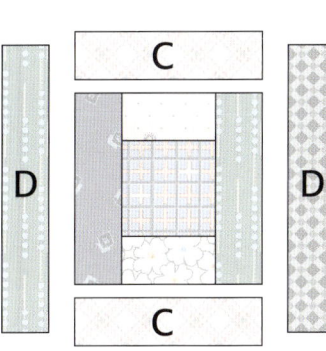
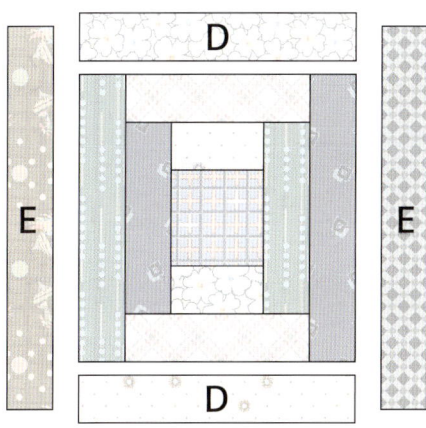

SEW

Lay out all patches to be sure you like the fabric arrangement.

Beginning with the light B strips, sew strips to opposite sides of the center A square in alphabetical order, alternating pairs of light and dark strips as you go. Finish with the dark E strips to complete the Courthouse Steps block.

A collection of Lizzy's playmates on Granny's quilt, from the Albright family photo album.

Designed by Ricky Tims

37 Dutchman's Puzzle

This dynamic block was among the first to be documented by the *Ladies Art Company*, as early as 1895. Alternate names for the design include Dutchman's Wheel, Windmill, and Wild Goose Chase.

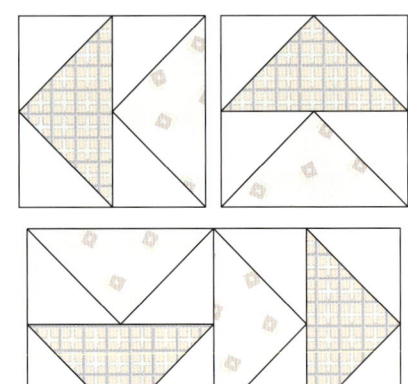

Dutchman's Puzzle Assembly

FABRICS NEEDED

Fabric 1 (dark): 6″ x 6″
Fabric 2 (medium): 6″ x 6″
Fabric 3 (light background): 10″ x 10″

CUT

Fabrics 1 and 2 – *cut from each:*
   1 square 5 1/4″ x 5 1/4″ ⊠ (A)
Fabric 3
   8 squares 2 7/8″ x 2 7/8″ ◻ (B)

SEW

Stitch B triangles to the adjoining short sides of each A triangle to make a total of 4 flying geese units each with fabrics 1 and 2 at their centers.

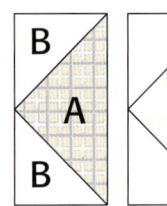

Sew a fabric 1 and a fabric 2 flying geese unit together to make a quarter-block. Make 4.

Sew 2 rows of 2 quarter-blocks each, watching orientation. Sew the rows together to make the Dutchman's Puzzle block.

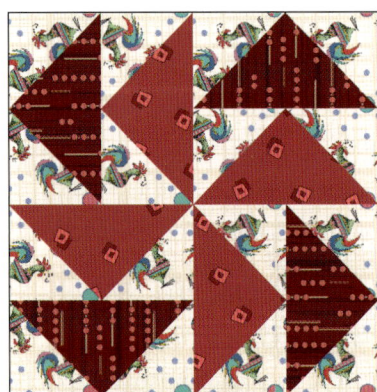

Dutchman's Puzzle Color Options

Granny's 1930 Sampler: From the Lizzy Albright Collection

Designed by Ricky Tims 101

38 Birds in the Air

Also known as Flying Birds, Flock of Geese, and Flight of Swallows, this quilt block was catalogued by Ruth Finley in her book *Old Patchwork Quilts and the Women Who Made Them* (1929), but it was used in quilts at least as early as the Civil War.

FABRICS NEEDED

Fabric 1 (background): 12″ x 12″
Fabric 2 ("birds"): 11″ x 11″

CUT

Fabric 1
  2 squares 4⅞″ x 4⅞″ ◨ (A)
  12 Template B
Fabric 2
  24 Template B

SEW

Stitch together fabric 1 and fabric 2 B triangles to make a pieced square. Make 12.

Arrange 3 rows using 3 pieced squares and 3 fabric 2 B triangles. Sew the rows, and then sew the rows together to make a pieced triangle. Make 4.

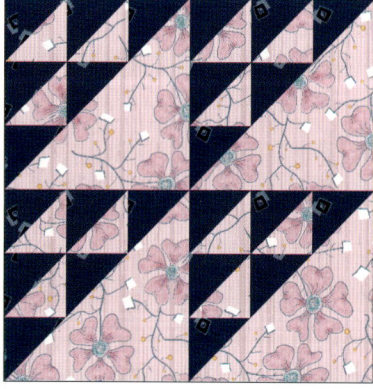  

Birds in the Air
Color Options

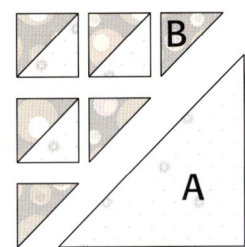

Birds in the Air Assembly

ALTERNATE CONSTRUCTION OPTION

If you prefer to make the small pieced squares two at a time, follow these steps:

Do not cut any B patches from fabric 1, and cut only 12 B patches from fabric 2.

Cut 6 squares 2½″ x 2½″ from both fabric 1 and fabric 2.

Draw a diagonal line on the wrong side of each of the 6 fabric 1 squares. Place fabric 1 and fabric 2 squares right sides together with marked fabric on top. Sew ¼″ from each side of the marked line. Cut apart on the marked line to make 2 pieced squares. Repeat the process to make 12 pieced squares total. Press well and then trim to size using Trimming Guide B.

Sew a pieced triangle to a fabric 1 A triangle to make a quarter-block. Make 4.

Sew 2 rows of 2 quarter-blocks each. Sew the rows together to complete the Birds in the Air block.

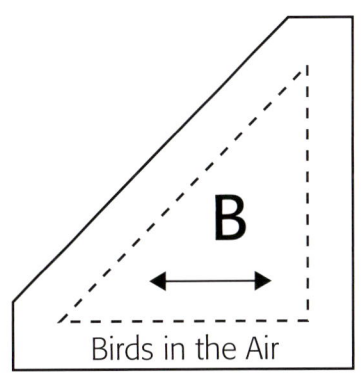

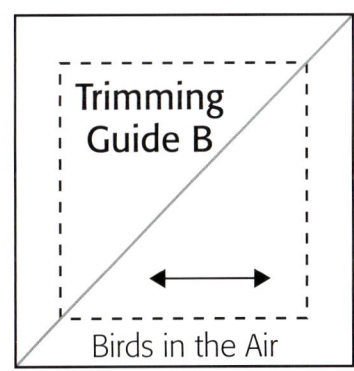

Designed by Ricky Tims

38 cont.

FROM THE PAGES OF
Lizzy Albright and the Attic Window, Chapter 24

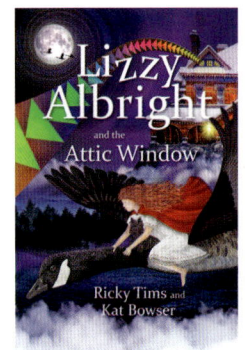

A thick, black cloud was boiling in the distance just above the treetops of Valendale.

"What do you think that is?" the guard asked. "It's not a fire—or at least I don't think it is."

The station mate focused his telescope and took a closer look.

"It's birds," he said, "one helluva lot of birds."

They monitored the swarm with great curiosity and were fascinated at how dense and organized the birds were. The churning mass was so far away, and moved so slowly, that it almost appeared to be stationary.

It eventually reached the edge of the forest, where it changed formation. The bottom descended to the ground, stirring up dust, while the top rose high into the air. The birds flew in circles, creating a vortex, which made them look more like a cyclone than a flock of grackles.

Designed by Ricky Tims

39 Double Wedding Ring

Published patterns for this classic block go back at least as far as 1928. It is one of the most recognizable of quilt patterns, and well worth the effort of piecing. It's a true showstopper!

FABRICS NEEDED

Fabric Group 1 (arcs): assorted prints totaling 12″ x 14″
Fabrics 2 and 3 (arc corners): 4″ x 4″ each
Fabric 4 (background): 13″ x 18″

CUT

Fabric Group 1 – *cut a total of:*
    56 squares 1½″ x 1½″ (areas 1 through 7)
Fabrics 2 and 3 – *cut from each:*
    4 Template A
Fabric 4
    1 Template C
    4 Template D
    4 Template B

OPTIONAL NOTE TO HAND PIECERS

The foundation pieced arcs and the A, B, C, and D patches can be sewn together by hand if you prefer, for beautiful accurate results and a relaxing sewing experience!

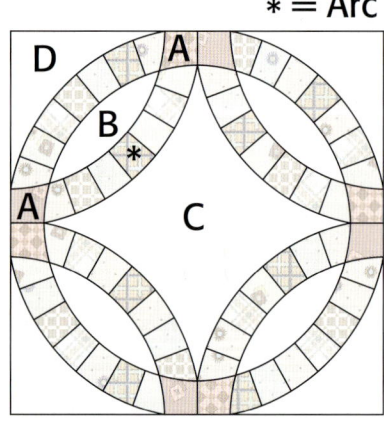

* = Arc

Double Wedding Ring Assembly

106   Granny's 1930 Sampler: From the Lizzy Albright Collection

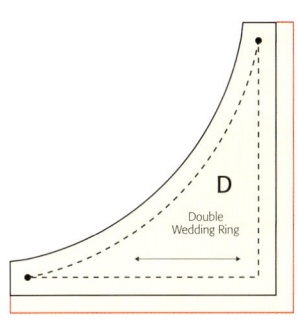

ALTERNATE CONSTRUCTION OPTION

Cut the straight edges of D slightly large and add to the block as directed. Then trim the block to 8½" square after assembly is complete.

SEW

Make 8 accurate paper copies of the arc foundation. Foundation piece the arcs. Trim edges even with outer lines on the foundation paper. Sew a line of stay stitching inside the outer seam allowances (about ⅛" from the raw edges). Carefully remove the foundation paper from the backs of the arcs.

Instructions for foundation piecing are on page 14.

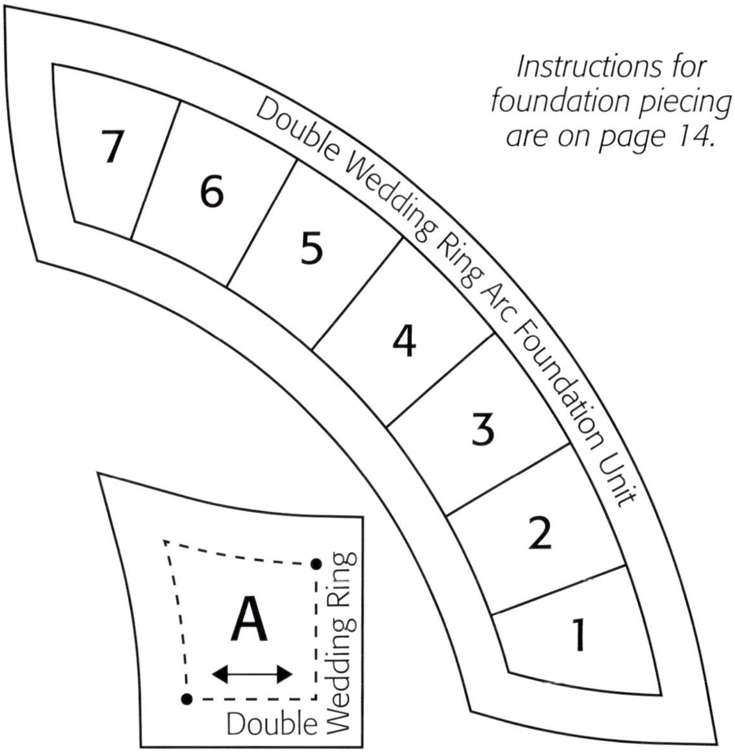

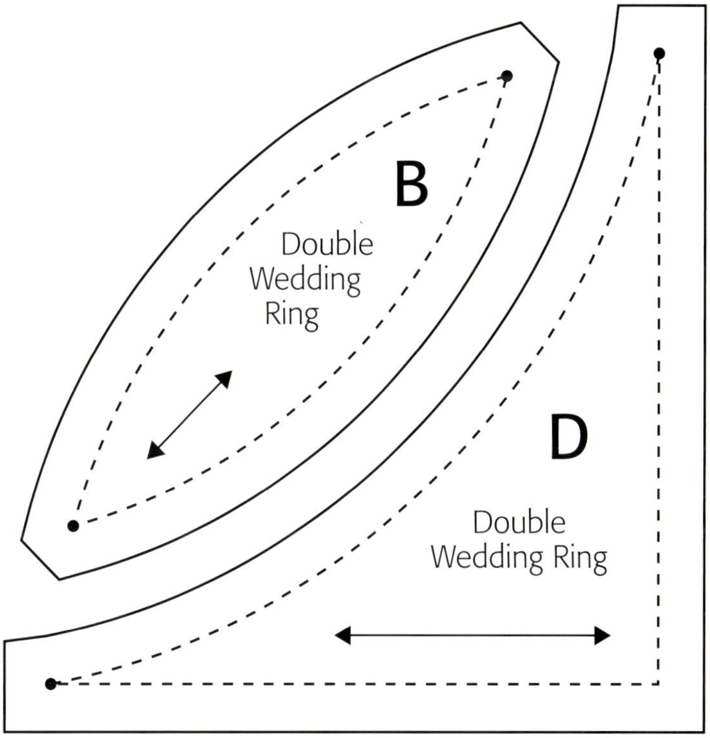

Designed by Ricky Tims   107

39 cont.

Sew 2 A patches, 1 of each fabric, to a foundation arc. Stitch B patch to a second foundation arc. Sew the 2 units together to make a "melon" unit. Make 4.

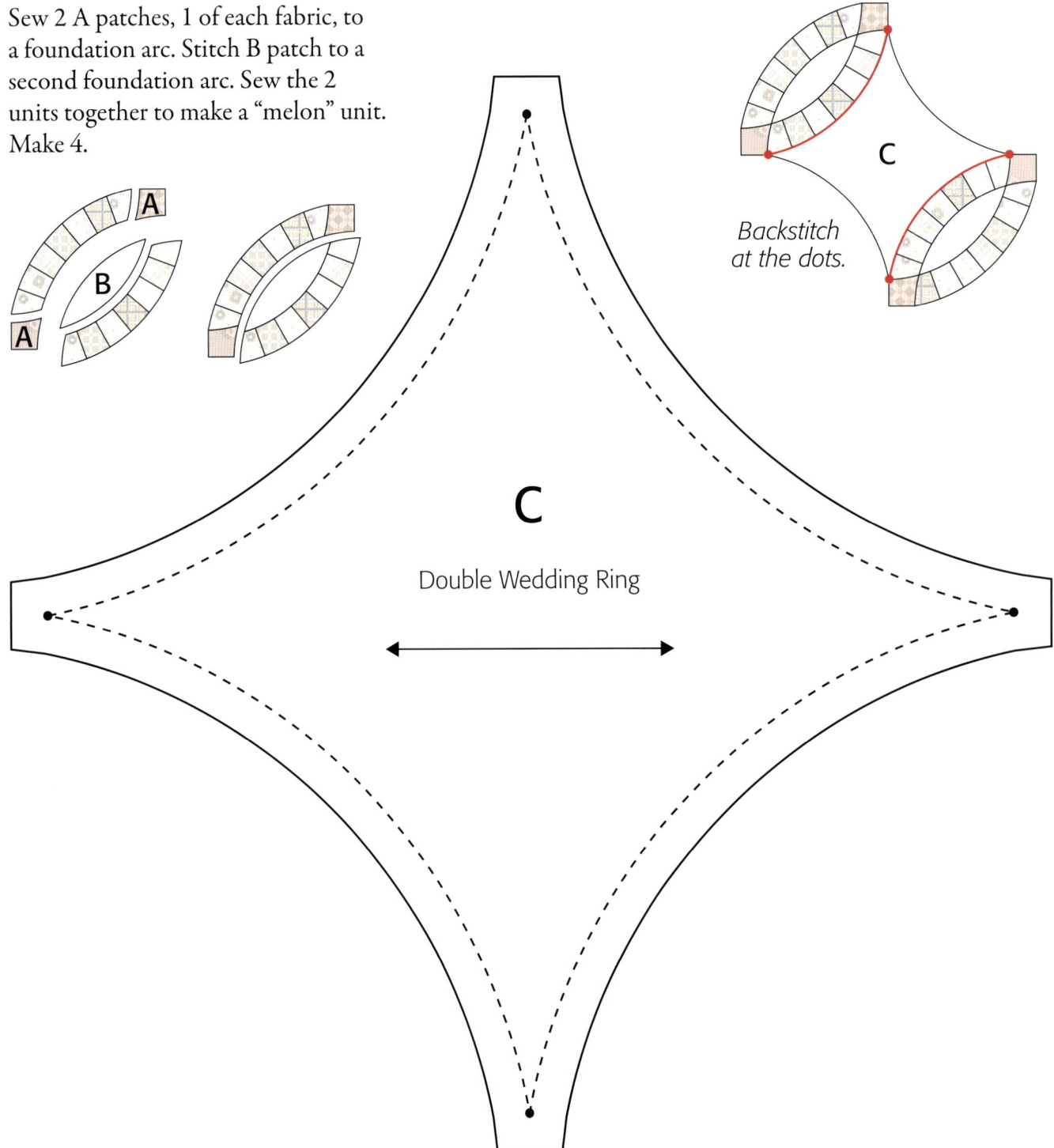

Backstitch at the dots.

C
Double Wedding Ring

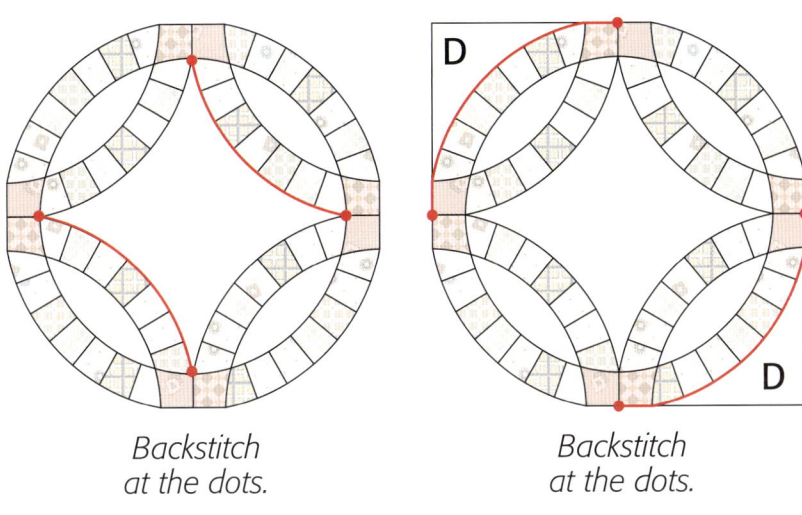

Backstitch at the dots.   *Backstitch at the dots.*

To assemble the block, begin by sewing melons to opposite sides of the C patch. Repeat to add melons to remaining sides of C.

Add a D to each corner and then stitch the 4 short seams between the melons to complete the Double Wedding Ring block. If you cut your D patches oversize, trim the block to 8½″ square.

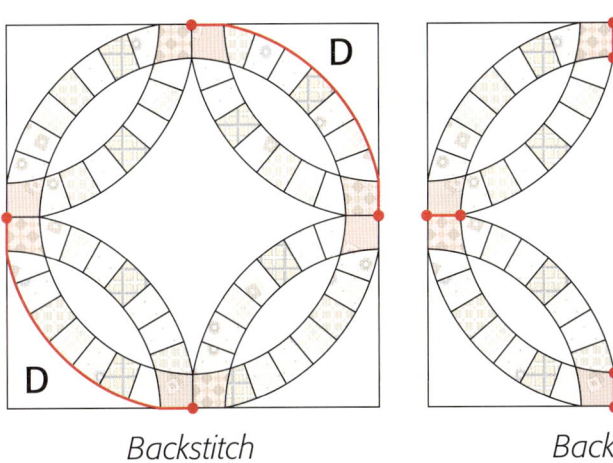

Backstitch at the dots.   *Backstitch at the dots.*

Double Wedding Ring Color Options

Designed by Ricky Tims

40 Log Cabin

Published patterns for this classic quilt block date back at least to the *Ladies Art Company* version of 1895. The block is simplicity itself; the magic lies in how multiples of the block can be set together to make virtually limitless designs. The Log Cabin block also owes much of its popularity to being a wonderful way to use up thin strips of scrap fabric. The center square is traditionally cut from a red fabric, to symbolize the fire at the heart of the home.

FABRICS NEEDED

Fabric 1 (center square): 3" x 3"
Fabric Group 2 (lights): assorted prints totaling 6" x 16"
Fabric Group 3 (darks): assorted prints totaling 6" x 18"

CUT

Fabric 1
  1 square 2½" x 2½" (A)

Fabric Group 2 – *cut a total of:*
  1 strip 1¼" x 2½" (B) *and* 1 matching strip 1¼" x 3¼" (C)
  1 strip 1¼" x 4" (D) *and* 1 matching strip 1¼" x 4¾" (E)
  1 strip 1¼" x 5½" (F) *and* 1 matching strip 1¼" x 6¼" (G)
  1 strip 1¼" x 7" (H) *and* 1 matching strip 1¼" x 7¾" (I)

Fabric Group 3 – *cut a total of:*
  1 strip 1¼" x 3¼" (C) *and* 1 matching strip 1¼" x 4" (D)
  1 strip 1¼" x 4¾" (E) *and* 1 matching strip 1¼" x 5½" (F)
  1 strip 1¼" x 6¼" (G) *and* 1 matching strip 1¼" x 7" (H)
  1 strip 1¼" x 7¾" (I) *and* 1 matching strip 1¼" x 8½" (J)

SEW

Lay out all patches to be sure you like the fabric arrangement.

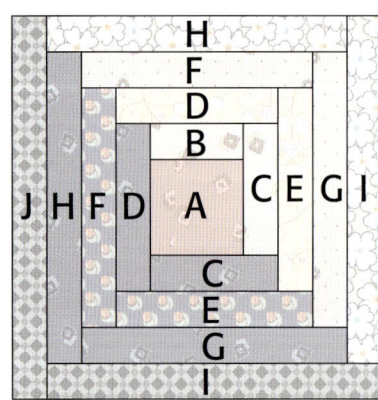

Log Cabin Assembly

ACCURACY TIP

To make sure your block is accurate and square, press well after adding each "round" of 4 strips. After round 1, the unit should measure 4" square from raw edge to raw edge. After round 2, it should measure 5½" square, after round 3 it should measure 7" square, and once completed the block should measure 8½" square.

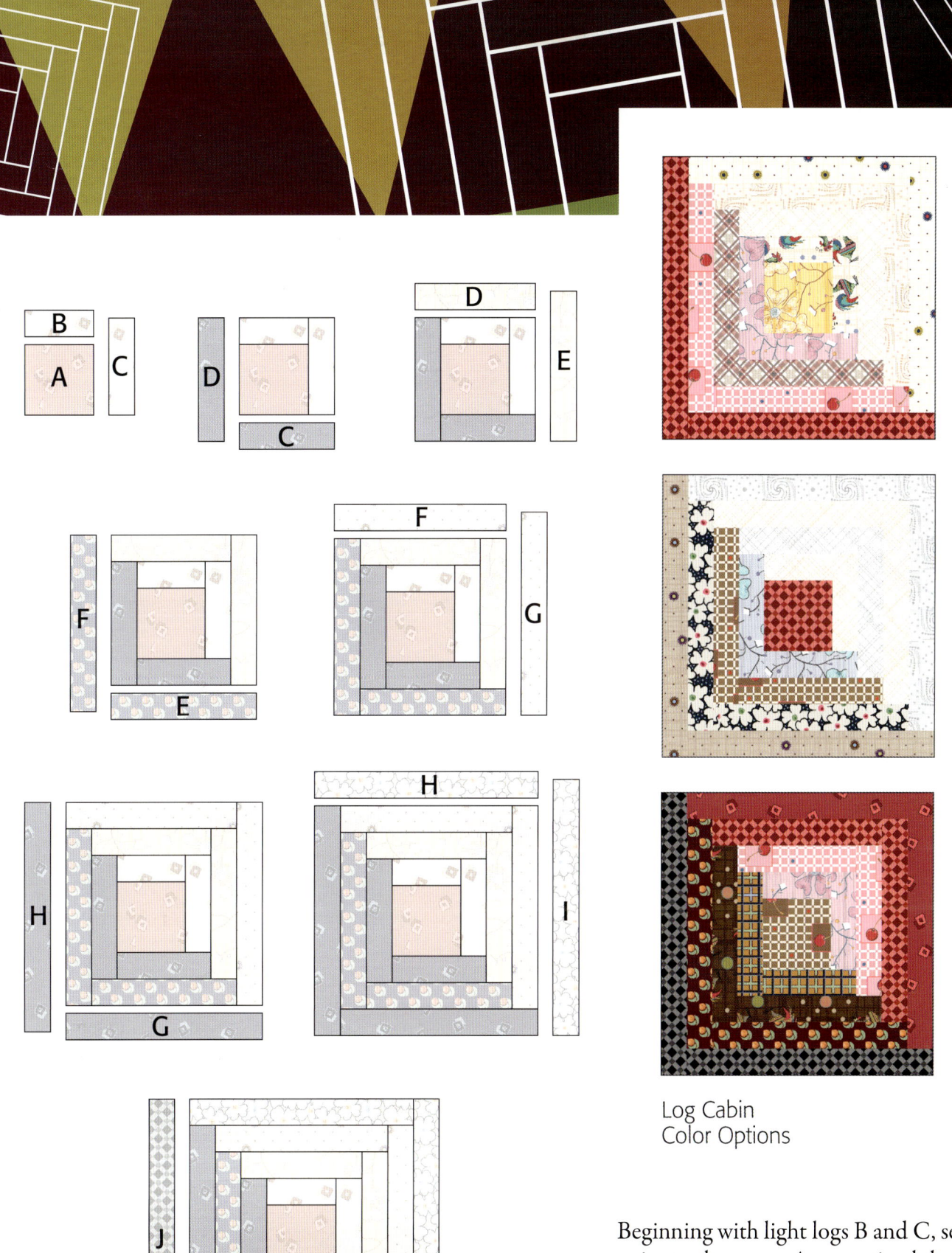

Log Cabin
Color Options

Beginning with light logs B and C, sew strips to the center A square in alphabetical order, alternating pairs of light and dark logs as you go. Finish with dark logs I and J to complete the Log Cabin block.

Designed by Ricky Tims 111

41 Broken Dishes

The *Ladies Art Company* published a pattern for this quilt block as early as 1895, and some sources credit its origin to the 1700s, so it's a true classic. Lizzy's grandmother may have known it by the name Old Tippecanoe.

FABRICS NEEDED

Fabric 1 (background): 10″ x 10″
Fabrics 2, 3, 4, and 5 ("dishes"):
    4″ x 7″ each

CUT

Fabric 1
    8 squares $2^{7}/_{8}$″ x $2^{7}/_{8}$″ (A)
Fabrics 2, 3, 4, and 5 – *cut from each:*
    2 squares $2^{7}/_{8}$″ x $2^{7}/_{8}$″ (A)

Broken Dishes Assembly

Broken Dishes Color Options

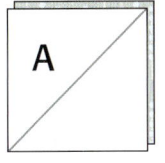 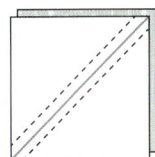 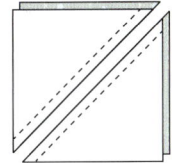

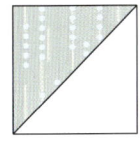 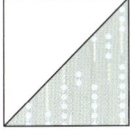

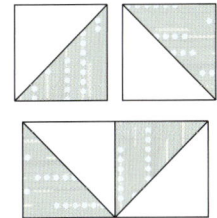

SEW

Draw a diagonal line on the wrong side of each fabric 1 square. Place fabric 1 and fabric 2 squares right sides together with marked fabric on top. Sew 1/4″ from each side of the marked line. Cut apart on the marked line to make 2 pieced squares. Repeat to make 4 pieced squares using each of fabrics 2, 3, 4, and 5. Press seams towards the darker fabrics.

Sew together 4 matching pieced squares to make a quarter-block. Make 4 total.

Sew 2 rows of 2 quarter-blocks each. Sew rows together to complete the Broken Dishes block.

FROM THE PAGES OF
Lizzy Albright and the Attic Window, Chapter 3

"Which china set should I put out this year?" asked Nellie. "I believe we've used the Currier & Ives set for the last couple of years."

"We have, and it's still my favorite, so I say we use it again this year." Granny paused a moment in thought. "Let's make it a Christmas Eve tradition. Currier & Ives every Christmas Eve," she said with a smile and a lilt in her voice as though she were breaking some rule of etiquette. This particular set of china had a decorative rim of green holly and red berries alternating with sprigs of mistletoe. Each plate had a different winter scene in the center. It was far more spectacular than the other two sets of Christmas china Granny had inherited.

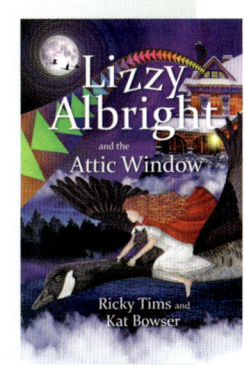

Designed by Ricky Tims

42 Kansas Dugout

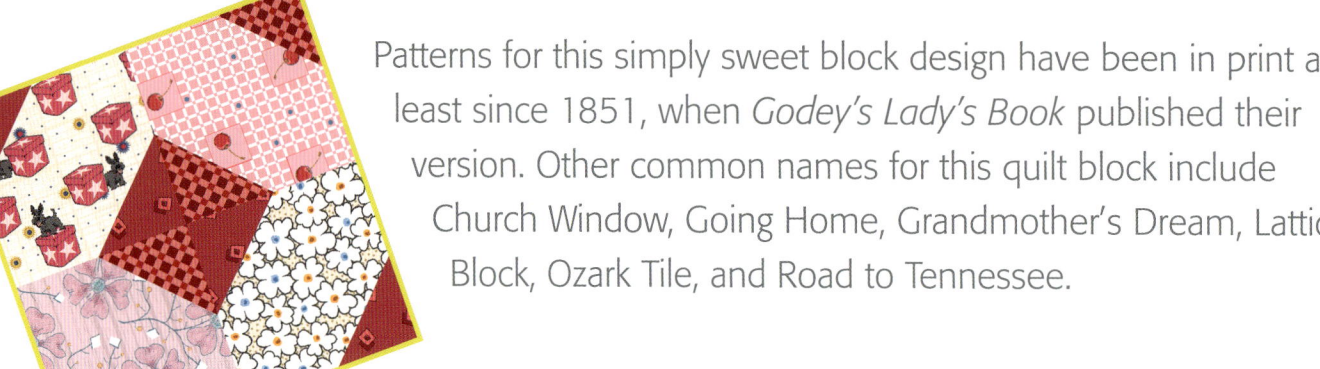

Patterns for this simply sweet block design have been in print at least since 1851, when *Godey's Lady's Book* published their version. Other common names for this quilt block include Church Window, Going Home, Grandmother's Dream, Lattice Block, Ozark Tile, and Road to Tennessee.

FABRICS NEEDED

Fabric Group 1 (lights): assorted prints totaling 10″ x 10″

Fabrics 2 and 3 (backgrounds): 6″ x 6″ each

CUT

Fabric Group 1 – *cut a total of:*
4 squares 4½″ x 4½″ (A)

Fabrics 2 and 3 – *cut from each:*
4 squares 2½″ x 2½″ (B)

SEW

Draw a diagonal line on the wrong side of each fabric 2 and fabric 3 B square. Place fabric 2 B squares on opposite corners of a fabric 1 A square, right sides together, aligning edges, and with Bs on top. Sew on the marked lines.

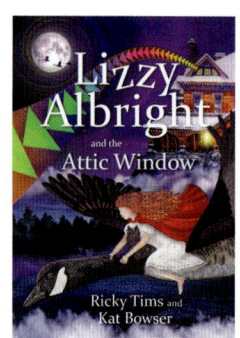

FROM THE PAGES OF
Lizzy Albright and the Attic Window, Chapter 13

"That, my dear, is Ansa, the royal city of our beloved Ailear. Our destination is just on the other side of the city."

Lizzy whispered to herself, "Ansa. Ailear." Though these names were unfamiliar, she thought they were beautiful. She slowly and deliberately repeated them again, "Ann-suh. All-air."

"If Ansa is a city, is Ailear a state, like Kansas?"

"Kansas?" replied McDoogle. "Ah, Lass, I'm fearful to tell ye, but I don't think we're in Kansas ony mair."

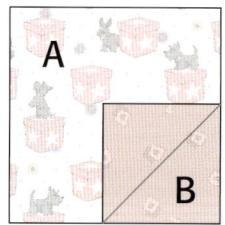
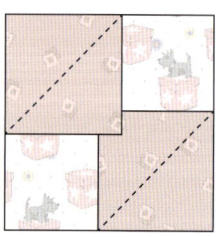

Granny's 1930 Sampler: From the Lizzy Albright Collection

Trim ¼" from seams. Press seams towards the corner triangles to complete the pieced square. Repeat to make 4 pieced squares total, 2 with fabric 2 corner triangles and 2 with fabric 3 corner triangles.

Referring to the Assembly diagram, sew 2 rows of 2 pieced squares each, watching orientation and placement of fabrics 2 and 3. Sew the rows together to complete the Kansas Dugout block.

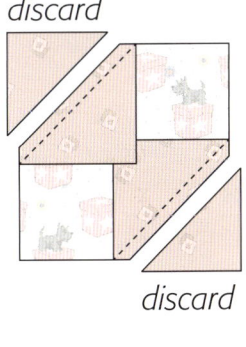
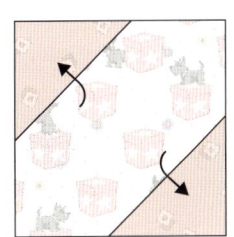

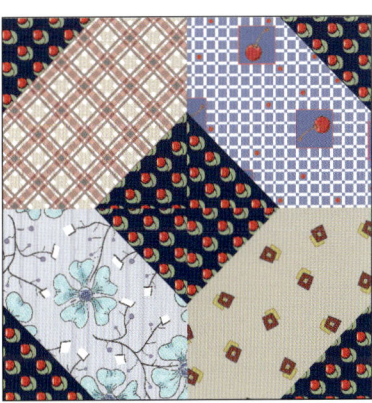

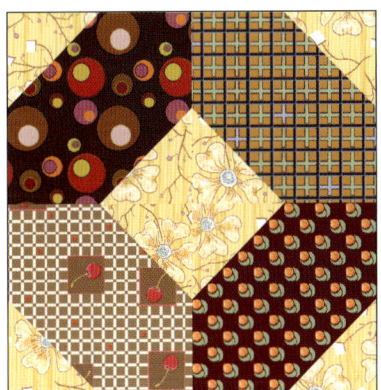

Kansas Dugout Color Options

Kansas Dugout Assembly

Designed by Ricky Tims   115

Quilt Assembly

FABRICS NEEDED

Fabric 1 (vertical sashing): 1 yard
Fabric 2 (horizontal sashing, outer border background, binding): 4 yards
Fabric 3 (outer border light triangles and corner diamonds): 1¼ yards
Fabric Group 4 (inner border dark triangles): assorted prints totaling 1½ yards
Fabric Group 5 (inner border light diamonds): assorted prints totaling ⅞ yard
Fabric Group 6 (outer border light nine-patch chain): assorted prints totaling 1 yard
Fabric Group 7 (outer border medium/dark nine-patch corners): assorted prints totaling 1¾ yards
Backing: 7½ yards

Note: You will also need 90″ x 99″ batting.

CUT

Fabric 1
    42 Template A (page 121)
Fabric 2
    10 strips 2½″ x width of fabric (binding)
    *60 squares 5⅝″ x 5⅝″ ◨ (D)
    16 squares 5¼″ x 5¼″ (F)
    42 Template B (page 121), cut on lengthwise grain
Fabric 3
    4 squares 10″ x 10″ (E)
    28 squares 6″ x 6″ ⊠ (C)
Fabric Group 4 – *cut a total of*:
    52 squares 4½″ x 4½″ ⊠ (Foundation 1 area 1, Foundations 2 and 3 areas 1 and 3)
    8 squares 3″ x 3″ ◨ (Foundation 1 areas 3 and 4)
Fabric Group 5 – *cut a total of*:
    108 squares 2½″ x 2½″ (all Foundations area 2)
Fabric Group 6 – *cut a total of*:
    **14 strips 1⅝″ x 15″
    **14 strips 1⅝″ x 8″
Fabric Group 7 – *cut a total of*:
    **28 strips 1⅝″ x 15″
    **28 strips 1⅝″ x 8″

*See Cutting Diagram, page 125.
**After cutting strips as listed, *trim* to exact width using Trimming Guide (page 124).

Goose Feathers Quilting

To fit inside the large triangles of the Flying Geese Outer Border.

Granny's 1930 Sampler: From the Lizzy Albright Collection

Quilt Assembly

Designed by Ricky Tims 119

Quilt Assembly

QUILT CENTER ASSEMBLY AND THE ATTIC WINDOW SETTING

To make the Attic Window sashing, sew a fabric 1 A strip to the left side of each of the 42 blocks, stopping and backstitching at the dot. Press seams towards the strips. Sew a fabric 2 B strip to the bottom of each block, stopping and backstitching at the dot. Press seams towards the strips. Sew each corner mitered seam, starting at the dot; press mitered seams towards the red fabric.

Arrange 7 rows of 6 blocks each. Sew the rows, and then sew the rows together to complete the quilt center.

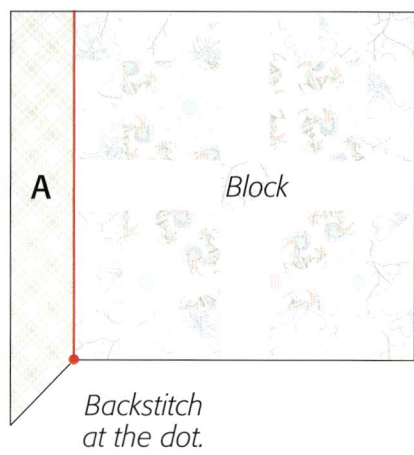

Backstitch at the dot.

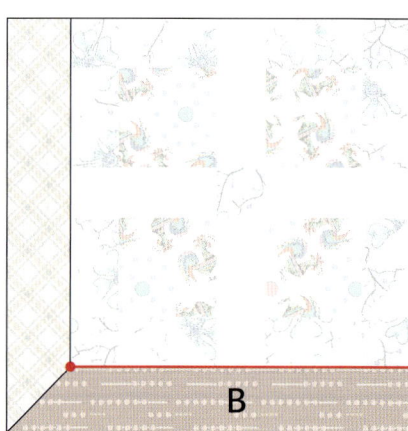

Backstitch at the dot.

Start sewing at the dot.

Quilt Center Assembly

120   Granny's 1930 Sampler: From the Lizzy Albright Collection

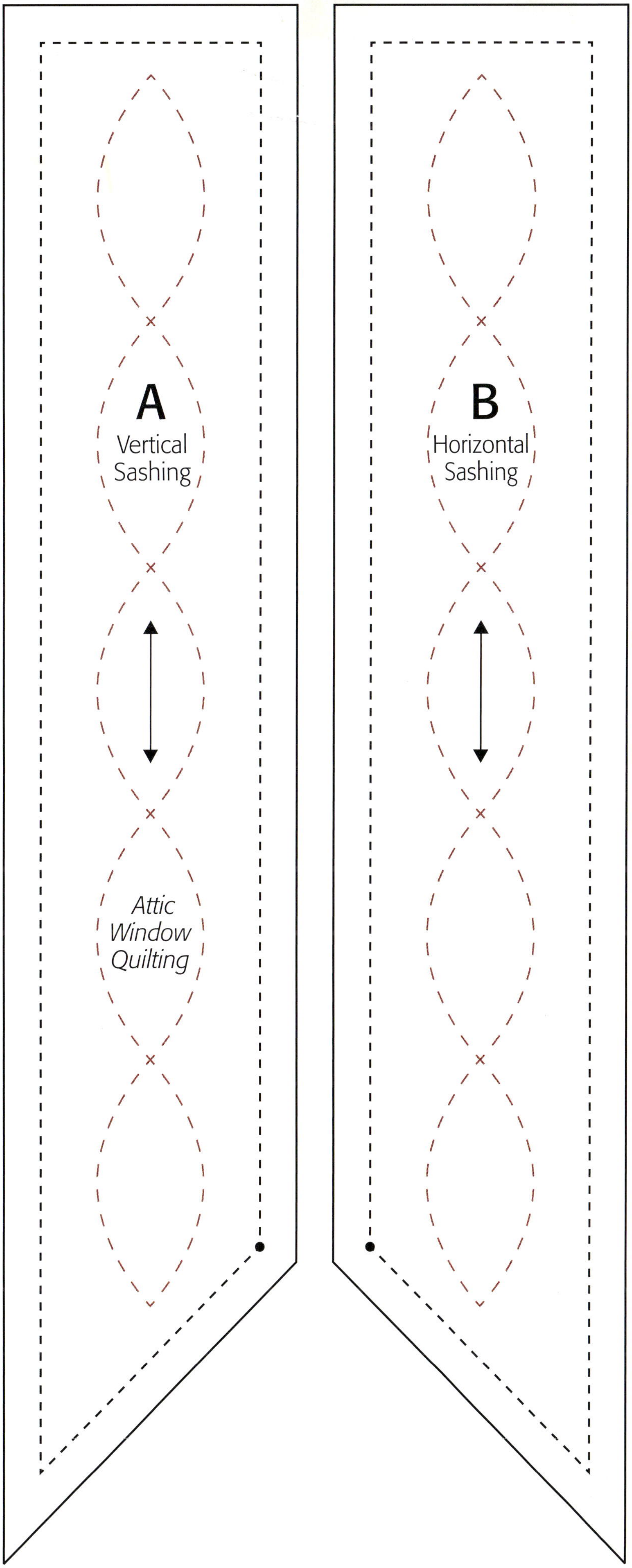

A Vertical Sashing

B Horizontal Sashing

Attic Window Quilting

FROM THE PAGES OF
Lizzy Albright and the Attic Window, Chapter 6

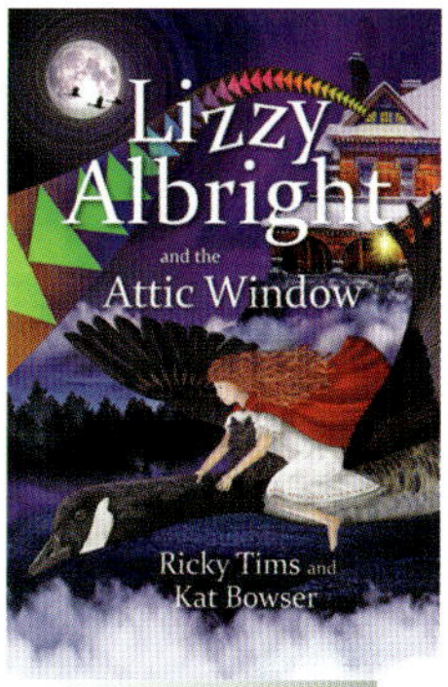

Granny asked, "Do you see how each block has a strip of fabric on the left side and another darker strip along the bottom?"

The question brought Lizzy back to reality. "I do," said Lizzy.

"When quilt blocks are sewn together like this, it's called an Attic Window setting. I saw nothing but a jumbled mess when I put my blocks side by side. But then I thought about trying the Attic Window, and it worked like magic!"

Lizzy stepped back and noticed that each quilt block appeared to have been placed inside of a window frame. It made her think about how every window on earth had a different view—and that outside of every window was a world of possibilities.

Designed by Ricky Tims

Quilt Assembly

DIAMOND INNER BORDER

Make 8 accurate paper copies of foundation 1, and 50 copies each of foundations 2 and 3. Foundation piece all the inner border units. Trim edges even with outer lines on foundation papers.

Sew together 2 units 1 and 13 each of units 2 and 3, alternating units 2 and 3, to make a side border. Make 2. Sew to the sides of the quilt center.

Sew together 2 units 1 and 12 each of units 2 and 3, alternating units 2 and 3, to make a top/bottom border. Make 2. Sew to the top and bottom of the quilt center.

Sew a line of stay stitching inside the outer seam allowance of the inner border (about 1/8″ from the raw edges). Carefully remove all foundation paper from the back of the border. Press well.

Unit 1   Unit 2   Unit 3

Instructions for foundation paper piecing are on page 14.

Foundations are reverse of finished unit.

Note: If you make 25 copies of page 123, and 8 copies of this page, you will have enough paper foundations 1, 2, and 3 for the inner border.

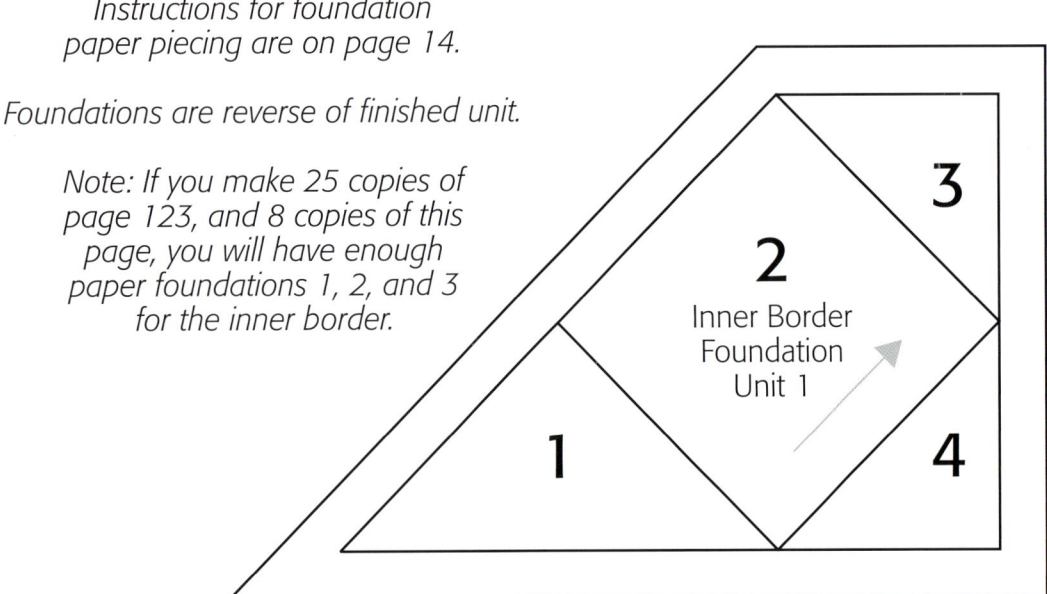

Inner Border Foundation Unit 1

Sides Inner Border

Top and Bottom Inner Border

122   Granny's 1930 Sampler: From the Lizzy Albright Collection

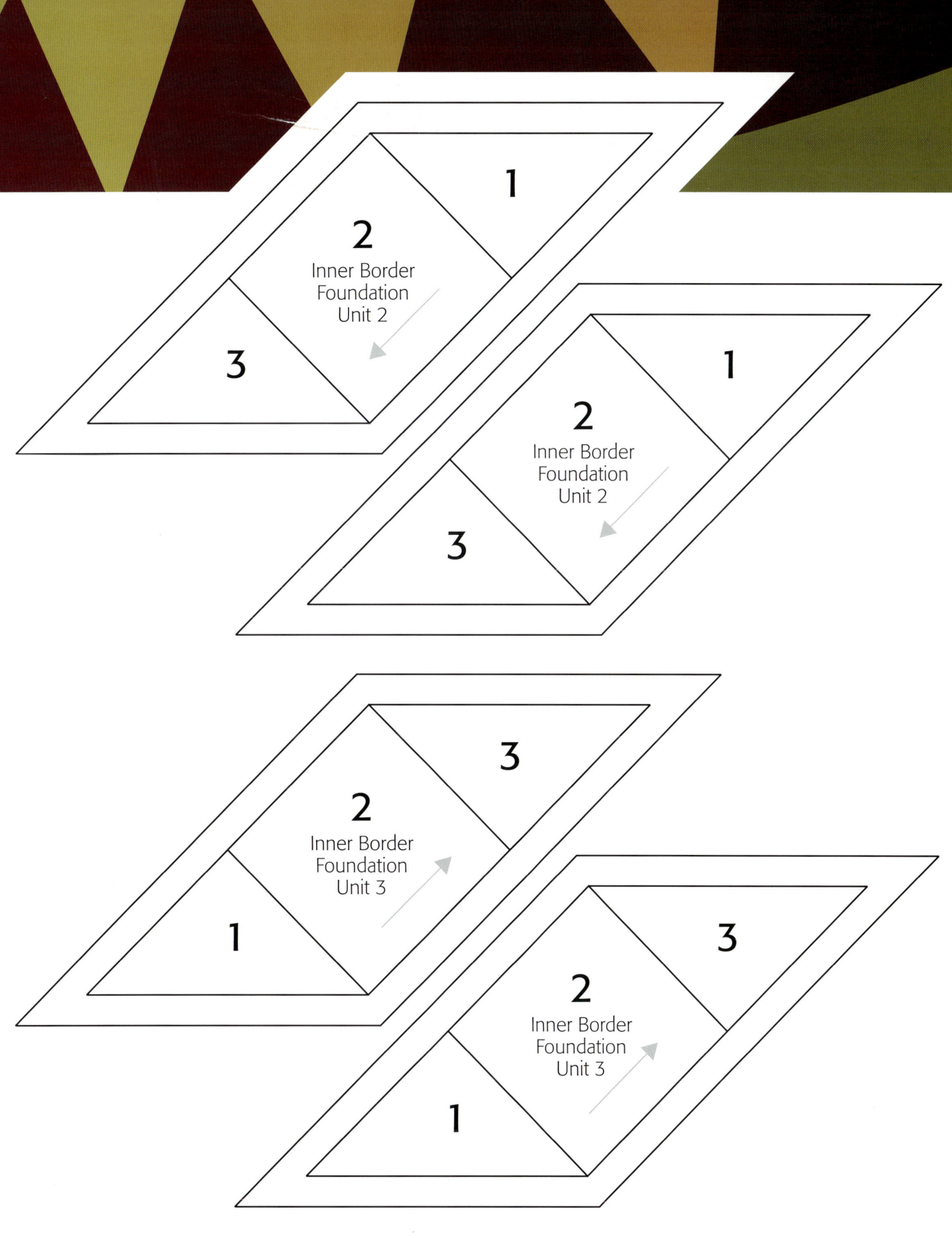

Designed by Ricky Tims 123

Quilt Assembly

FLYING GEESE OUTER BORDER

Sew a fabric 6 trimmed long strip and 2 fabric 7 trimmed long strips together to make strip set A. Make 14 total. Sew a fabric 7 trimmed short strip to each side of a fabric 6 trimmed short strip to make strip set B. Make 14 total.

Strip Set A

  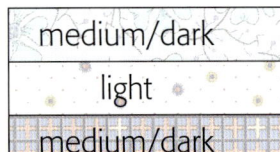

Strip Set B

Trimming Guide A/B

Border
Geese
Nine-Patch

FROM THE PAGES OF
Lizzy Albright and the Attic Window, Chapter 6

"There are geese in my quilt. Look at the border!"

Lizzy pulled the quilt closer and grabbed the edge.

"These are called Flying Geese. They are triangles that chase after each other all going in the same direction." Lizzy ran her hand around the different colored triangles in the border and easily understood why they were called Flying Geese.

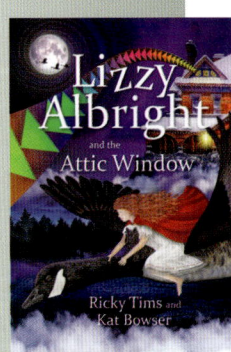

From each strip set A, cut 8 segments using Trimming Guide A for the exact width. From each strip set B, cut 4 segments in the same way. You should have a total of 112 A segments and 56 B segments.

Sew together 3 segments, A, B, and A rotated, to make a nine-patch. Make 56 total.

Nine-Patch

Sew fabric 3 C triangles to 2 adjoining sides of a nine-patch, making sure the lightest patches are oriented as shown. Make 56 total nine-patch triangle units.

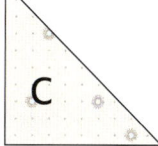

Note diagonal position of light chain.

USING A STRIPED FABRIC

Note: Lizzy's grandmother was careful to orient the striped fabric in her outer border units (and the horizontal sashing strips) all in the same (horizontal) direction. Follow the next instructions carefully to do the same.

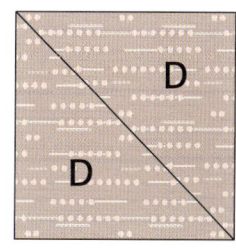
Cut 30

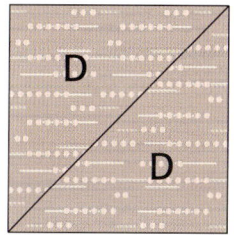
Cut 30

Cutting Diagram

Stitch fabric 2 D triangles to corners of the nine-patch triangle units, watching orientation of the stripe. Make 30 border flying geese of the first type shown below, and 26 of the second type. You will have 8 fabric 2 triangles left over.

Make 30

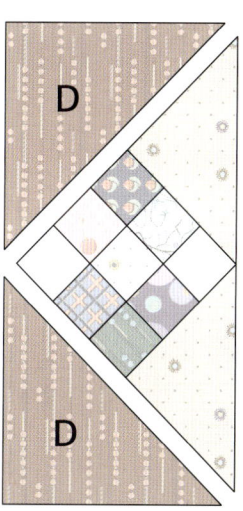
Make 26

Designed by Ricky Tims

Quilt Assembly

BORDER CORNER UNITS

Draw diagonal lines on wrong sides of 4 fabric 2 F squares, watching orientation of lines carefully. Place marked squares on opposite corners of a fabric 3 E square, right sides together, aligning raw edges and watching orientation. Sew on marked lines; trim seams to $1/4"$. Press seams towards triangles. Place marked squares on remaining corners of unit, sew on marked lines, trim seams to $1/4"$, and press seams towards triangles to complete a border corner unit. Make 4.

Sew together 15 border flying geese to make a side border. Make 2. Sew to the sides of the quilt, watching orientation.

Sew together 2 border corner units and 13 border flying geese to make a top/bottom border. Make 2. Sew to the

Border Flying Geese

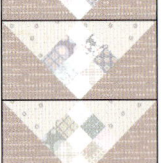

Side Border

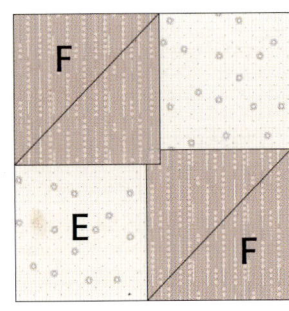
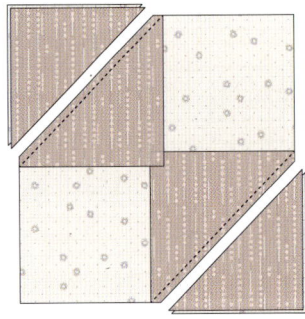
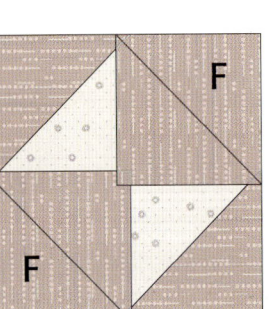
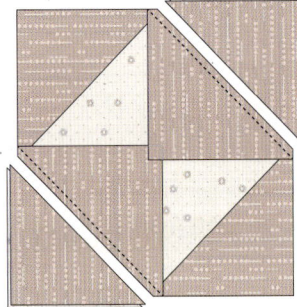
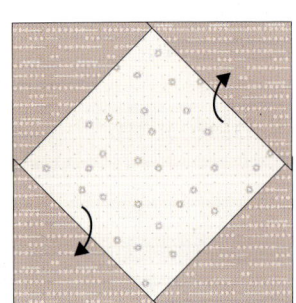

Border Corner Unit

126 Granny's 1930 Sampler: From the Lizzy Albright Collection

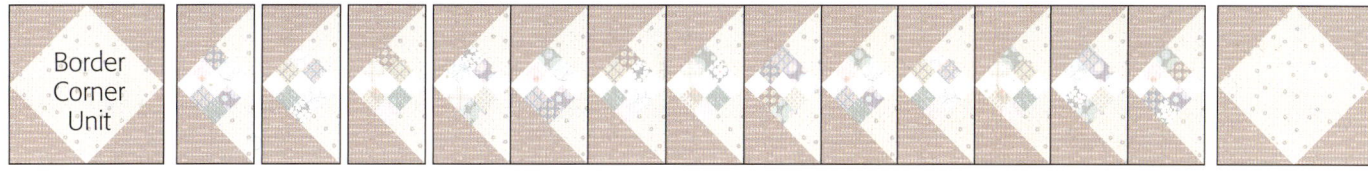

Top/Bottom Border

top and bottom of the quilt, watching orientation.

Sew a line of stay stitching inside the outer edges of the quilt (about 1/8″ from the raw edges).

QUILTING AND FINISHING

Layer, baste, and quilt. Lizzy's grandmother's quilt was hand quilted, which was the most common way to quilt during those days. Much of the quilt is quilted in the ditch, or stitched a quarter-inch in from seams. There is crosshatching on a 45° angle as well as vertical and horizontal. A few decorative designs are included in the quilt (see the sashing design on page 121 and a goose feather motif on page 118), and echo quilting is appropriate in places. Use the images in this book for your quilting design inspiration.

Bind with the 10 width-of-fabric strips cut from fabric 2.

Designed by Ricky Tims

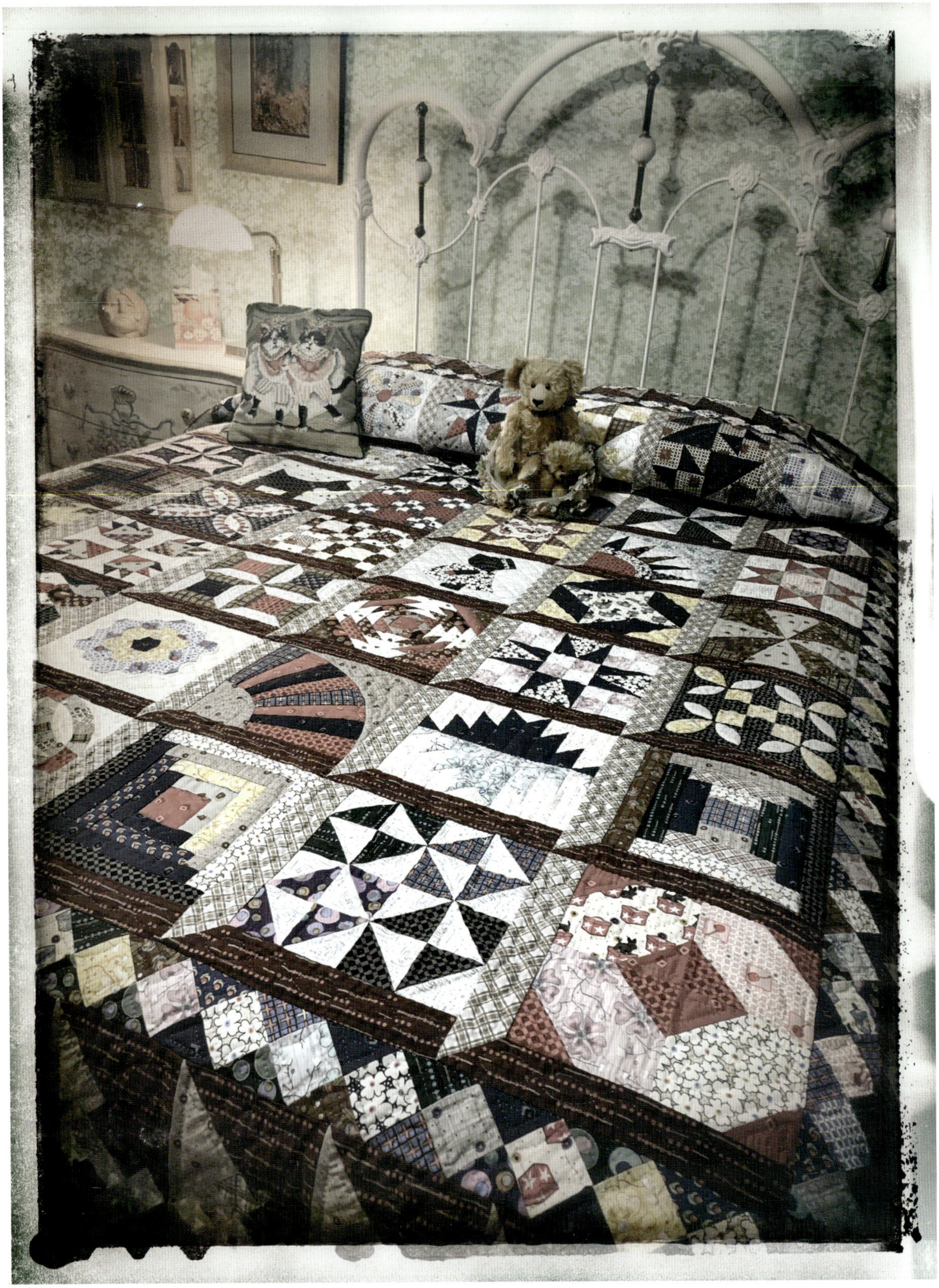

Photographed in the home of Judith Baker Montano.

Lizzy's room in the McHale mansion, from the Albright family photo album.